BR

THROUGH
OLOGY

THE SCIENCE OF PRIORITIZING AND IGNORING FOR MAXIMUM SUCCESS

BROOKS ALLISEN

Breakthroughology: The Science of Prioritizing and Ignoring for Maximum Success

Brooks Allisen

Madeson Publishing

Allisen Consulting Ltd.

Nanaimo, BC, V9T 6P9

ISBN Number: 978-0-9813678-8-0 (Paperback)

ISBN Number: 978-1-0693147-0-3 (Hardcover)

ISBN Number: 978-0-9813678-9-7 (eBook)

Connect & Inspire...

I thank you for embarking on this journey with me to escape the overwhelm trap and unlock your true potential. Once you have read this book, and if you found value in Breakthroughology, I would greatly appreciate it if you'd take a moment to share your insights by leaving a review. Your feedback is invaluable in helping other true achievers and entrepreneurs discover these transformative principles and life-changing methods. One review from you could be the lifeline someone needs. Right now, they're drowning in tasks – just like you once were. Thank you.

Go Here to Leave Your Review

https://breakthroughologybook.com/reviews

Introduction: About the Author

Brooks Allisen has been an entrepreneur for over 50 years, focusing on alternative healing, essential oils, business, and psychology.

Along the way, he noticed a big problem: professionals today are drowning in tasks and information.

To help, he created the Breakthrough Blocker Method—a simple, effective system to cut through the chaos, focus on what matters, and actually get things done.

His goal? To help people succeed without burning out, so they can enjoy their work and their life.

Other Books by Brooks Allisen:

The Calm Within: Releasing Trauma, Anxiety, Stress, and Fear Using Natural Therapies – ISBN-13: 978-0981367873

Vegetarian Diet Plan: Just What You Need – ASIN: B00CCK61RW

The Journey Behind the Method

As you delve into "Breakthroughology," I invite you to explore a different perspective—not the usual author's details, but rather some guiding principles that can enrich your experience with this book's content. These principles have helped me navigate challenges and seize opportunities throughout my journey. With over six decades of insights gained from both the commercial world and life's path, I believe understanding certain core concepts can enhance your ability to implement the methods outlined in this book.

In this section, I will share my thoughts on four essential pillars—Intent, Belief, Perseverance, and Integrity—that serve as the backbone of the philosophy I've learned over the years. Each concept has been instrumental in shaping my approach to prioritizing what truly matters and learning to ignore distractions that derail progress. Through personal anecdotes and insights gained from years of observation, I hope to deepen your understanding of how these principles can illuminate your path to maximum success.

Intent

Intent is the concept of seeing, in your mind's eye, what you want to accomplish in a given situation.

Having lived on the prairies all my life, one Christmas my wife, our kids, and I visited the west coast for a vacation. When we left Alberta, it was -40º C/F (really cold) with two feet of snow on the ground. When we landed on Vancouver Island, it was +10º

C/50º F, and instead of snow—there was lush green grass! Our kids' immediate response was, "We're moving here!"

During our vacation, we all fell in love with the ocean—the views, the beaches, the trees, the feeling of being so close to nature – and the weather! It felt so comfortable and peaceful to listen to the waves rolling in and crashing on the beach. We loved the smell of the ocean and forest, and the cool, moist breezes. Heading back over the mountains, to the frozen flatlands where we lived, we vowed to find a way to move to the coast and be close to the ocean, maybe even have an ocean view. That commitment set our intention and put the wheels in motion for the move to Vancouver Island.

Intent can result from an experience as well as an idea. Ideas are born in the ether and can lie dormant for years, or they can become the impetus for immediate action. Either way, intent or intention is the spark that launches your journey to get the results you want at some point in the future. The first step on your path to maximum success is setting your intention.

Belief

Belief is the process of building on an intention—it's the next step in making a vision or idea a solid reality.

Over the next six months, we made several applications for jobs on Vancouver Island and made numerous 600-mile trips over the mountains for in-person interviews. During the July long weekend, we drove to Victoria for a job interview for my wife. Unfortunately, this wasn't successful. When we got home and checked the answering machine (this was in the pre-mobile phone era), there was a message for me about a job interview in Nanaimo, also on Vancouver Island. I called the employer to explain we had just been on the island, and the soonest I could return would be the following month, during the August long weekend.

Before heading to Vancouver Island for the August long weekend, we decided to have the flooring updated throughout our house. While we were away, the flooring team installed carpet and sheet vinyl in half the house. I successfully landed the job in Nanaimo, and during our stay, we worked with a Realtor to find a house. The real estate market was extremely tight and nothing on MLS interested us. Fortunately we discovered a for-sale-by-owner property where a deal had just fallen through. The house perfectly fit our needs and we bought it. While still in Nanaimo, we secured mortgage approval and arranged for our Realtor to handle the purchase details – with a move-in of September 1st.

Upon returning home, we had the flooring team complete their work the next day. I placed a For Sale By Owner sign on our front lawn, and within an hour, we had a cash offer for the full asking price—did I mention the real estate market was squeaky tight? Over the next few weeks, we handled all the arrangements for our house sale, rented a truck, and transported our furniture and car to Nanaimo—just in time for the kids to start school.

At this point, our intent to move to Vancouver Island had propelled us forward, and our unwavering belief had resulted in remarkable manifestations: finding a house in Nanaimo and selling our Alberta home. While our new house didn't have an ocean view, we were living within a mile of a swimmable sandy beach.

Perseverance

Perseverance is more than just holding onto a dream—it's doing whatever is needed to make your dream come true.

Over the next few years, we embraced island life fully, exploring Vancouver Island, swimming, and playing in the ocean. We took scuba diving lessons and enjoyed boat trips to nearby islands, particularly Gabriola Island with its charming Saturday craft and home-bake market. Our adventures took us to the rugged west coast of Tofino and Ucluelet, and included a memorable day trip on the MV Lady Rose from Port Alberni to Bamfield. Among our ventures was buying and renovating an apartment in Victoria with our kids, which we later sold for a modest profit.

Our dream of having an ocean view never wavered. After viewing countless houses without finding the right one, we purchased a vacant ocean-view lot. The property presented unique challenges—triangular in shape with the wide part facing the street and a dramatic 60% slope over 90% of its area. This meant designing a level-entry home with multiple lower levels. After consulting a Feng Shui expert and creating preliminary sketches, we engaged an architectural designer. I obtained my general contractor's license to self-build our new house using ICF (Insulated Concrete Forms) blocks—an innovative choice that gave us solid concrete walls from foundation to roof.

The construction journey tested our resolve. ICF construction was virtually unknown to local framers at the time, and our first framer's poor work had to be corrected before finding someone to complete the framing. Despite challenges with both framers, I managed to get the project to lock-up stage with roof, doors, and windows installed – at this point we were a full year into the build.

Our Ocean View House

Finding reliable sub-trades proved easier for electrical, plumbing, insulation, exterior stucco, and heating. Serendipitously, both a skilled drywaller and an experienced finishing carpenter approached me on-site when I needed them most. Though the first framer's errors meant some exterior walls weren't quite square with each other, requiring careful adjustments during finishing, the end result was beautiful. After two years of perseverance through trying times, we had our ocean-view house, just a block from the beach.

Three Levels of Our Ocean View House

We enjoyed our 4,000 sq ft, three-level home with eight bedrooms and six bathrooms for a decade before downsizing to a more practical one-level, three-bedroom home closer to amenities. Our children have built their own lives—our daughter became a teacher, married, and has two high-school-aged girls, while our son serves in the Canadian Navy near Victoria, married with two elementary-school boys who love hockey.

Integrity

Integrity means remaining faithful to your original dream while building upon it to create the life you've always envisioned.

We've called Nanaimo home for over 32 years now, and our adventures have expanded far beyond Vancouver Island. From diving the Great Barrier Reef off Australia's northeast coast to exploring Antoni Gaudí's magnificent Sagrada Familia in Barcelona, we've embraced global experiences. We even purchased and renovated a two-bedroom apartment in Cuenca, Ecuador, enjoying regular vacations there for over 11 years. Our timeshare has enabled affordable international holidays in numerous countries.

It all begins with a dream and an intention to create a wonderful life. Progress comes when you believe that everything you do builds toward that dream. Remember that your dream life will materialize as long as your vision remains solid, you persevere, and you maintain unwavering belief that what you're living for is always within reach. You can manifest whatever you dream—you just need that initial dream or idea as your starting point. Your dream is your reality—so have fun along the way!

Prelude: Breaking Free from the Overwhelm Trap

What if the key to achieving more is actually doing less?

The modern professional's life is a paradox. We find ourselves constantly adding more tasks to our already overwhelming to-do lists, hoping that by doing more, we will ultimately achieve more. Yet, despite all our hustle and dedication, true progress often remains just out of reach. It's easy to mistake the frenzied pace of our daily activities for real, meaningful achievement, but as we'll explore, busyness and breakthrough success are far from synonymous.

The truth is, being "busy" can be a dangerous trap—one that leaves us exhausted, unfulfilled, and still yearning for that elusive sense of forward momentum. Breaking free from this cycle requires a new approach to productivity, one that prioritizes the essential and allows you to ignore the noise. We begin by introducing a powerful new paradigm—the Breakthrough Blocker Method—to help you shift your focus from quantity to quality, and transform your approach to success.

The Modern Professional's Dilemma: Drowning in Tasks, Thirsting for Progress

Every morning, millions of professionals wake up and dive into their workday, armed with a steaming cup of coffee and an endless list of tasks. They tick boxes, reply to emails, attend meetings, and hustle to finish their projects—yet by evening, the sense of accomplishment they crave remains elusive. Instead of feeling fulfilled, many end the day with a mix of frustration and exhaustion, only to find themselves adding even more to the list for tomorrow. The irony is painfully evident: the harder they work; the further real progress seems to slip from their grasp.

The core of this problem lies in our obsession with "doing more." We believe that by tackling as many tasks as possible, we can eventually reach the pinnacle of our careers and enjoy the success we've always dreamed of. But this approach has a major flaw: **it confuses movement with advancement**. Think about it—a hamster wheel is full of movement, yet it leads absolutely nowhere. In a similar vein, filling our schedules to the brim keeps us in a state of constant action, but it rarely results in meaningful breakthroughs.

The pressure to do it all, be it all, and respond to everything can leave you feeling powerless. We're taught that productivity means checking off every box on our to-do lists, regardless of how many boxes there are or how trivial they might be. Instead of defining our days by their impact, we define them by how busy we are—but at what cost? This relentless drive often comes at the expense of our health, well-being, and, paradoxically, our most important goals. The key lies not in getting more things done but in getting the **right things** done.

The Myth of Doing More: Why Busyness Doesn't Equal Breakthrough

Let's address a major misconception right away: **Busyness does not equal productivity**. There's a difference between working hard and working smart. Unfortunately, modern society has ingrained in us the idea that if we're not constantly in motion, we're falling behind. This myth has become so pervasive that many people wear their busyness like a badge of honor—proof that they're working hard, making sacrifices, and deserving of success.

But let's pause for a moment and consider the reality behind that badge. When was the last time you looked back at your week and felt genuinely proud of the progress you made toward something truly significant? For many, those moments are rare. Instead, we feel bogged down, our energy spread thin across a myriad of responsibilities that, in hindsight, may not have mattered all that much. The truth is, doing more can dilute our focus to the point where we're actually achieving less.

Consider some of history's most impactful figures—think of inventors, artists, and business leaders. What they all have in common isn't an obsession with doing everything; it's an obsession with doing what matters. They understood that true productivity is about focusing on the few critical actions that will yield the most significant results. They ignored the distractions, the unnecessary demands, and instead channeled their energy toward their most meaningful pursuits. **Their success was not a result of doing more—it was a result of doing less, but doing it better.**

Introducing the Breakthrough Blocker Method: A New Paradigm for Success

This book is about helping you break free from the overwhelm trap by adopting a different mindset. Imagine what your career could look like if you could focus purely on the tasks that move the needle—the ones that propel you forward, help you grow, and bring you genuine satisfaction. This is what the Breakthrough Blocker Method is all about.

The Breakthrough Blocker Method encourages a radical shift: from trying to do **everything** to strategically ignoring the noise and focusing on what really matters. It's a system designed to help you identify and eliminate the obstacles standing in the way of your biggest breakthroughs—the "blockers" that hold you back from achieving your fullest potential. By learning to block out distractions and say "no" to tasks that drain your energy without adding value, you can regain control of your time and finally start making real progress.

This is not about abandoning hard work—far from it. It's about channeling that hard work into the areas where it will have the most impact. Imagine if every action you took throughout your day brought you closer to a major goal, rather than simply keeping you busy. Imagine having the clarity to know exactly where to direct your efforts, and the confidence to ignore everything else. That's the kind of transformation the Breakthrough Blocker Method aims to deliver.

Your 30-Day Journey to Clarity, Focus, and Career-Defining Achievements

If you've ever felt overwhelmed by your workload or struggled to make meaningful progress, you're not alone—and you're not stuck. The Breakthrough Blocker Method is a framework designed to guide you on a 30-day journey that will help you redefine how you approach your professional life. Over the next month, you'll learn to identify which tasks truly matter, which ones can be ignored, and how to structure your days to maximize impact rather than output.

The journey starts by understanding the true cost of overwhelm. Many people don't realize just how much their productivity—and ultimately, their happiness—is sabotaged by trying to do too much. We'll explore what's driving this culture of overwhelm and how it keeps you from achieving the breakthroughs you deserve. Then, using the CLEAR framework, you'll learn how to Categorize your professional commitments, List and prioritize what really matters, Eliminate the unnecessary, Act on your priorities, and Refine your approach.

The Cost of Overwhelm: The Hidden Price You Pay

The cost of living in a constant state of overwhelm is immense. It's not just about the exhaustion at the end of a long day; it's about what that exhaustion takes away from you in the long run—opportunities, creativity, and the ability to seize moments that could define your career. Chronic overwhelm leads to decision fatigue, which in turn diminishes your ability to discern what truly matters. When you're constantly bouncing between minor tasks, you're robbing yourself of the energy you need to engage in deep, meaningful work.

It's time to break free. It's time to acknowledge that not everything on your list deserves your time, and it's time to focus on the few things that do. This approach may feel counterintuitive, especially in a culture that celebrates hustle above all else, but it's the secret to transforming how you work and how you experience your career.

The Breakthrough Blocker Method in Action

Let's take a look at how this can apply in real life. Imagine a high-level marketing manager named Sarah. Like many of us, Sarah's days were filled with back-to-back meetings, countless emails, and a laundry list of tasks that left her feeling constantly behind. She was overworked and overwhelmed, and yet, deep down, she knew that most of what she was doing wasn't leading to the kind of career-defining achievements she had always envisioned.

When Sarah started using the Breakthrough Blocker Method, everything began to change. She learned to categorize her commitments, making it clear which ones were truly contributing to her long-term goals and which were simply keeping her busy. She prioritized the key initiatives that aligned with her career aspirations and began eliminating tasks that had little to no impact on her progress. It wasn't easy—saying no felt uncomfortable at first—but over time, Sarah found herself with the space to focus on what really mattered. The result? Not only did Sarah start making real progress towards her biggest goals, but she also found herself less stressed, more energized, and genuinely enjoying her work again.

This transformation is possible for you, too. It starts by questioning everything on your plate. Ask yourself: *Is this task genuinely important, or is it just urgent?* The distinction is critical. The Breakthrough Blocker Method helps you identify and eliminate the tasks that feel urgent but don't truly contribute to your growth, allowing you to focus your energy where it counts.

Why You Need a New Approach to Productivity

Our current understanding of productivity is fundamentally flawed. We live in a society that measures success by the number of things we can accomplish in a day—regardless of their significance. But true productivity isn't about checking boxes—it's about creating value. It's about understanding that **more does not always mean better**, and that sometimes, the most powerful thing you can do is to choose not to do something.

The Breakthrough Blocker Method is about reclaiming your time and using it intentionally. Imagine being able to wrap up your workday knowing you've made genuine progress, rather than simply having survived another day. Imagine a work life that doesn't require constant firefighting but instead allows you to build, create, and grow. This is what happens when you prioritize quality over quantity—when you break free from the overwhelm trap and embrace a more focused approach.

Overcoming the Fear of Letting Go

One of the biggest challenges you'll face in this journey is learning to let go. Many of us cling to busyness because, on some level, it makes us feel productive and in control. Saying no can feel like admitting failure, or like we're letting someone down. But letting go is not about failure—it's about freedom. Freedom to focus, freedom to create, and freedom to truly excel in the areas that matter most.

The fear of letting go is real, but the rewards are worth it. By eliminating the noise, you give yourself the gift of clarity. You free yourself to dedicate time and energy to the projects and goals that will have the most impact. Remember, **you don't need to do everything to be successful—you just need to do the right things**.

The Road Ahead

As you embark on this journey, be prepared to challenge long-held beliefs about productivity. You may need to unlearn some of the habits and mindsets that have kept you in the overwhelm trap for so long. But take heart—this process is about empowering yourself to make decisions that serve your long-term growth and happiness.

Throughout this book, you'll learn practical techniques for implementing the Breakthrough Blocker Method in your own life. You'll discover how to categorize your commitments, identify your top priorities, strategically eliminate distractions, take decisive action, and continuously refine your approach. This journey will help you reclaim control over your professional life, allowing you to focus on what truly matters and achieve the breakthroughs you've been yearning for.

By the end of these 30 days, you'll have the tools to approach your career with a renewed sense of clarity and purpose. You'll know how to ignore the unimportant, prioritize the essential, and most importantly, experience a profound transformation in both your professional achievements and your personal well-being.

Get Ready to Break Free from Overwhelm...

In chapter one, we'll take a closer look at the root causes of overwhelm and how it manifests in our professional lives. You'll learn to recognize the signs of chronic overwhelm and understand why traditional approaches to productivity often fail to deliver the results you want. Together, we'll take the first step towards diagnosing and dismantling the overwhelm epidemic that keeps so many of us from reaching our true potential.

Contents

1. The Overwhelm Epidemic 1
2. Mapping Your Mental Clutter 9
3. Unmasking Your Priority Blindspots 19
4. The Breakthrough Blocker Revolution 29
5. The CLEAR Path to Breakthrough 39
6. Categorize: Mapping Your Professional Landscape 51
7. List Priorities: Defining Your North Star 65
8. Eliminate: Mastering the Art of Strategic Ignorance 75
9. Act: From Decision to Breakthrough 85
10. Refine: Evolving Your Breakthrough Strategy 93
11. Accelerating Your Success Flywheel 103
12. Navigating Career Complexities 113
13. The Breakthrough-Driven Leader 123
14. Breakthrough Balance: Integrating Work and Life 133
15. The Perpetual Breakthrough Mindset 141

16. Breakthrough Influence: Becoming an Industry Catalyst 153
17. Mastering Career Pivots and Transitions 163
18. The Future of Work: Thriving in an Age of Disruption 175
19. Conclusion: Your Breakthrough Legacy 183
20. Appendices 193

Chapter One

The Overwhelm Epidemic

Chronic overwhelm has become the silent killer of career progress.

Modern professionals are caught in an endless cycle of busyness that feels productive but, in reality, leaves them treading water. The constant bombardment of tasks, emails, and obligations creates a false sense of accomplishment, masking the fact that true breakthroughs remain just out of reach. The purpose of this chapter is to guide you to recognize the symptoms of chronic overwhelm that hold you back, understand the hidden costs of misplaced priorities, and learn why traditional time management methods simply aren't cutting it anymore.

It's time to recognize how this silent epidemic affects your productivity and blocks your path to success.

Recognizing the Signs of Chronic Overwhelm in Your Career

When you wake up already feeling behind, it's a red flag. The day hasn't even started, and there it is—a sinking feeling in your gut as you remember all that you have to do. Overwhelm doesn't announce itself dramatically. Instead, it creeps in slowly, settling into your morning thoughts, weighing down your energy, and making you feel like you're constantly sprinting but getting nowhere. You start the day with a to-do list, but by midday, that list has exploded into an unmanageable mess, leaving you frazzled. This cycle doesn't just affect your productivity at work; it spills over into your personal life too. When you feel overwhelmed, it's hard to switch off at home, making you less patient with loved ones, distracted during family time, and unable to fully enjoy your personal space. The constant mental strain means you're physically present but mentally absent, leading to strained relationships and a sense of disconnection from the people who matter most.

One of the clearest signs of chronic overwhelm is this sensation of perpetual exhaustion. It's not just about physical tiredness; it's emotional fatigue, mental clutter, and the sense that no matter how much you do, there's always more to be done. The brain, constantly flooded with tasks, loses its capacity to prioritize effectively. The clarity that should guide decision-making gets lost in the fog of too much to do and too little time to do it. This exhaustion doesn't just end when the workday is over—it comes home with you. It affects your ability to relax, to unwind, and to enjoy simple moments with family. Chronic overwhelm drains the joy from personal experiences, leaving you too depleted to fully participate in the non-work aspects of life that are supposed to recharge you.

Another key indicator of overwhelm is the feeling that you're constantly reacting. Instead of steering your career with purpose, you're bouncing from one urgent email to the next, putting out fires but never building something lasting. Your actions feel dictated by others' demands—like a calendar that keeps filling itself without your input. This is a trap that far too many ambitious professionals fall into, and recognizing it is the first step towards change.

Overwhelm isn't just unpleasant; it's a thief that steals from your long-term success. Acknowledging its presence is essential to reclaim control over your career.

The Hidden Costs of Misplaced Priorities

Busyness isn't the same as being effective. Too often, we wear our busy schedules like a badge of honor. We feel validated by the number of meetings we attend, the back-to-back calls, the miles-long email threads. But here's the truth: just being busy isn't moving you forward—it's keeping you stuck. The relentless drive to "do more" often comes at the cost of true progress. This kind of busyness distracts you from your real goals and prevents you from focusing on the bigger picture. Instead of making meaningful advances in your career, you're bogged down by the day-to-day struggle of balancing administrative tasks, client demands, interruptions, and project emergencies, which keeps you feeling exhausted rather than accomplished.

Moreover, this constant busyness creeps into your personal life in a destructive way. You may find yourself too mentally drained to engage with your family, struggling to be present during conversations, or just too tired to enjoy your hobbies. The burden of unfinished tasks doesn't stop at the office door; it follows you home, making it impossible to truly disconnect and recharge. This cycle makes it harder to cultivate happiness in your personal life, ultimately affecting your relationships and overall well-being.

The hidden costs of misplaced priorities are subtle but powerful. First and foremost, misplaced priorities rob you of opportunity. Imagine spending weeks working diligently on something, only to realize later that it had little impact on your overall goals. It's demoralizing. More importantly, it steals time away from what genuinely could have propelled you to the next level. By focusing on low-impact tasks, you forfeit time that could have been invested in learning a new skill, creating something impactful, or strategically planning the next step in your career.

This misalignment doesn't only affect your career; it also takes a toll on your personal life. When your energy is spent on trivial work, you have less to give to your loved ones and less time to engage in activities that bring you joy. The evenings that could have been spent recharging are often spent worrying about unfinished, unimportant tasks, leaving you in a perpetual state of stress. This creates a snowball effect where both your professional and personal life suffer, making it even harder to maintain a healthy balance or derive fulfillment from either area.

Additionally, misplaced priorities hurt your well-being. Constantly juggling tasks without pausing to assess their true importance is draining. The toll isn't just on your productivity but also on your mental health. Burnout doesn't come solely from hard work—it comes from working hard on the wrong things. The physical exhaustion combined with the disappointment of feeling like you're not achieving what you want can create a vicious cycle that's hard to escape. This mental and emotional fatigue doesn't stop when you leave work. You might find yourself constantly replaying unfinished tasks in your mind or feeling guilty for not doing enough, which not only saps your energy but also diminishes the quality of your time with family and friends.

The cost of misplaced priorities is not only what you do but also what you fail to do. By focusing on the wrong things, you end up missing out on real opportunities for career-defining breakthroughs. This problem doesn't just affect your work—it spills into your personal life too. When you're stressed about work priorities, you have less energy for family and friends. You might miss important moments or find yourself mentally absent even when you're physically home. Eventually, this takes a toll on your happiness and satisfaction with life. The consequences can be subtle at first—like feeling disconnected during dinner with your family—but over time, they grow into significant barriers to a happy, balanced life. You might find yourself with strained relationships, feeling distant from the people who matter most, and struggling to find joy in the small moments that once brought you peace.

Why Traditional Time Management Fails High-Achievers

Time management is broken when it comes to those with high aspirations. The calendars, productivity apps, and col-

or-coded planners promise efficiency, but they often overlook the core issue: you can't manage time if you don't know what matters most. Traditional time management strategies encourage people to "get more done," but they don't teach you how to choose the right things to do in the first place. This is the core flaw—focusing on quantity rather than quality. You could spend your entire day checking off tasks, but without understanding what truly deserves your attention, you might still be no closer to achieving meaningful progress. Many tools and methods fail because they're simply aimed at organizing tasks rather than helping you decide which ones are genuinely worth your effort. Without this critical filter, you end up investing your energy in things that yield little reward, leaving you with the illusion of productivity rather than real results.

High-achievers face a specific set of challenges. You're driven, you care deeply about your career, and you want to make an impact. But the very qualities that make you ambitious also make you vulnerable to overwhelm. The problem is that traditional time management assumes that all tasks are created equal—that with enough planning, you can squeeze everything in. But you can't. Not if you want to go beyond mediocrity. Ambitious people are often perfectionists who are driven to prove themselves, which means they're more likely to take on too much. They have a hard time saying 'no' because they believe they can handle it all, but this can lead to burnout. Without learning to distinguish what truly matters, high-achievers risk wasting their energy on trivial tasks that don't move the needle, ultimately leaving them overworked and underfulfilled.

The problem with old-school time management is that it doesn't help you distinguish between "urgent" and "important." Not everything that demands your attention deserves your attention. High-achievers don't just need efficiency; they need strategy. Without a strategic approach, your calendar fills up, your to-do list grows, and suddenly you're just trying to survive each day without a plan for thriving. High-achievers need a system that helps them focus on tasks that contribute to their long-term goals rather than getting caught up in the daily grind. It's not just about fitting tasks into your day; it's about making sure those tasks align with your broader vision of success. By focusing on what's truly important, you can start to clear the clutter and make room for meaningful progress, rather than just scrambling to get through another day. You need to be intentional with how you allocate your time, understanding that success isn't about volume—it's about impact.

To achieve breakthrough success, you need to learn a new approach—one that focuses not on managing time but on identifying and committing to the right priorities.

The Call to Recognize Overwhelm and Reclaim Your Career

This chapter has laid out the reality of overwhelm—how it sneaks into our careers and grows until it's stealing our potential. The next step in this journey is to equip yourself with a method to break free. The Breakthrough Blocker Method is designed to challenge the status quo of "doing more" and instead guides you to choose what's most impactful.

If you've recognized yourself in these pages, understand that this isn't the end—it's the beginning. There's a better way to work and live, one where overwhelm doesn't dictate your potential. Let's move forward with that in mind, one step closer to true breakthroughs.

Mental Clutter and Blocks Next...

We'll explore how to map out the mental clutter and identify the specific blockers that are preventing you from making significant progress.

"You don't have to be the best at everything.
You just have to be the best at what matters most."
– Unknown

Chapter Two

Mapping Your Mental Clutter

The path to clarity starts by understanding what currently stands in your way.

When your tasks and responsibilities are scattered across sticky notes, emails, and mental lists, it's impossible to see where your time is truly going. In this chapter, we're going to help you map all that mental clutter so you can begin to make sense of what you're carrying—and what you can start letting go.

The idea here is simple but powerful: You can't manage what you can't see. Many high achievers are overwhelmed simply because they've never paused to look at the sheer volume of what they've taken on. By creating a comprehensive task inventory, you'll gain a bird's-eye view of everything on your plate—and that's the first step toward reclaiming your time and energy.

Conducting a Comprehensive Task Inventory

The first key to mapping your mental clutter is to get it all out in the open—every last task, responsibility, and obligation. You might think you already know what you need to do, but until you see it all laid out in front of you, there's no real way to understand the depth and breadth of your commitments.

Step 1: Brain Dump Everything

Start by setting aside an uninterrupted hour. Find a quiet place, open your notebook, or a new document on your laptop or computer, and list every single task that's been bouncing around in your head. This is not the time to organize or prioritize—it's just about creating a complete inventory – it's just brainstorming ideas and thoughts. Don't censor yourself. If it's something that's weighing on your mind—whether it's work-related, personal, or even mundane—write it down.

- **Work tasks:** All your ongoing projects, meetings you need to plan, presentations to prepare, and emails you need to respond to.
- **Personal responsibilities:** Family events, errands, bill payments, and anything else demanding your attention.
- **Aspirations:** Think about those things you've put off, like picking up a hobby, or enrolling in a professional

course.

The beauty of this step is that it gets everything—literally everything—out of your head. Once you can see it all, you'll be able to deal with it. The more detailed you are, the better equipped you'll be to make meaningful changes.

Step 2: Organize and Categorize

Once you've brain dumped your entire mental clutter, it's time to organize it. Categorizing tasks can help you understand the different areas that demand your energy. Some common categories might include:

- **Urgent vs. Important:** Is this task something that needs your attention right now? Or is it something that's valuable in the long term?
- **Work vs. Personal:** It's crucial to see how balanced (or imbalanced) your time is between your career and your personal life.
- **Quick Wins vs. Projects:** Are these things that can be tackled in a few minutes, or do they require ongoing effort?

Categorizing helps you see patterns. Are most of your tasks related to work, leaving little room for personal care? Are urgent tasks eating up all your time, leaving you unable to work on what really matters for your long-term success?

Step 3: Identify the Commitments

Every item on your list is a commitment—something you've decided to dedicate time and energy to. Take a moment to reflect on the commitments you've identified. Are they all still valid? Sometimes we hold onto things out of habit, not because they align with our current goals or needs. Understanding where your commitments lie is key to uncovering what's contributing to your mental clutter.

Identifying Energy Drains and Productivity Black Holes

Once you've completed your task inventory, the next step is to identify those sneaky, often invisible energy drains—the activities that are eating away at your focus without contributing much value. Recognizing these black holes is critical to reducing overwhelm and making space for what really matters.

Step 1: Categorizing Energy Levels

Next to each task on your list, assign a simple label that reflects the impact this task has on your energy:

- **Energy-Boosting:** These are tasks that make you feel good when you complete them—they add value and give you a sense of accomplishment.

- **Neutral:** Tasks that just need to be done but don't drain you or energize you.
- **Energy-Draining:** The tasks that make your heart sink just thinking about them. They deplete you.

Energy-draining tasks are like slow leaks in your productivity tank. They need to be managed because they will quietly but consistently sap your capacity to do meaningful work.

Step 2: Calculate the Cost of Black Holes

Energy-draining tasks often become productivity black holes—they consume not only your energy but also time and mental space. Take a moment to reflect on how much time you spend on these draining activities. If a task takes hours to do but gives you little value in return, that's a black hole. Recognizing these tasks is the first step in managing them more effectively—by either eliminating them, delegating them, or learning to say "no" to them altogether.

Step 3: Decide What to Let Go

It's not enough to identify energy drains; the next crucial step is deciding what to do about them. Are there tasks that you can offload to someone else? Can you simply decide not to do some of them at all? Letting go can be difficult—sometimes we feel obligated to complete something because it's "on the list." But remember, if it's not adding value and it's draining you, it's more than fair to eliminate it.

The Art of Distinguishing Between Urgent and Important

A major contributor to overwhelm is failing to distinguish between tasks that are urgent and those that are important. Urgency often masquerades as importance, tricking us into putting out fires rather than building towards our goals.

Step 1: Understand the Difference

- **Urgent tasks** are things that demand immediate action. They are often linked to someone else's priorities rather than your own. For example, an email from your boss, a last-minute meeting, or a phone call that interrupts your deep work.

- **Important tasks** are those that contribute to your long-term goals and vision. They may not scream for attention right now, but they are the things that, if done consistently, will drive meaningful progress in your career and life.

Step 2: Plot Your Tasks on the Urgent-Important Matrix

The Urgent-Important Matrix, also known as the Eisenhower Matrix, is a simple but effective tool for categorizing your tasks:

1. **Urgent & Important**: Do these tasks immediately.
2. **Not Urgent but Important**: Schedule time for these tasks.
3. **Urgent but Not Important**: Delegate these if possible.
4. **Not Urgent and Not Important**: Consider eliminating these tasks.

Mapping out your tasks in this matrix helps you see, at a glance, which activities are worth your time and which are merely distractions. It also forces you to confront a tough reality—many of the tasks you're treating as priorities aren't actually that important in the grand scheme of things.

Step 3: Act on the Insights

After plotting your tasks, it's time to act on the insights you've gained. Focus your energy on the important but not urgent activities—this is where breakthroughs happen. These are the tasks that move the needle in your career, the ones that often get neglected because they don't have an immediate deadline. By consciously prioritizing these, you'll begin to see real progress.

Key Takeaway: Pinpoint Specific Blockers Preventing Career Breakthroughs

By the end of this chapter, you'll have a clear map of your mental clutter—a comprehensive inventory of every task, responsibility, and obligation. You'll know exactly which tasks are draining your energy and which ones are genuinely contributing to your progress. This awareness is the key to breaking free from overwhelm.

Once you've identified your energy drains and mapped out the difference between urgency and importance, you'll have the clarity you need to pinpoint the specific blockers that are holding you back. These blockers—whether it's saying "yes" to everything or being stuck in the cycle of urgent tasks—are what we'll address in the upcoming chapters.

The clearer you are about what's on your plate, the easier it will be to make decisions about what stays, what goes, and what needs to be prioritized. The journey to success starts with seeing things as they are—only then can you transform them into something better.

Blindspots Next...

With your mental clutter mapped and your key blockers identified, it's time to take the next step in your journey—discovering the blindspots in your current approach to prioritization. In the next chapter, we'll look at how to unmask the hidden habits and assumptions that are preventing you from making the breakthroughs you need.

"If you want to have a good life,
you have to stop doing the things that don't matter."
- Joshua Becker
(Author and advocate of minimalism)

Chapter Three

Unmasking Your Priority Blindspots

The way we prioritize shapes not only our careers but our entire lives.

We often think we know what's important, but the truth is, many of us are unknowingly sabotaging our potential by focusing on the wrong things. Without clear prioritization, we end up reacting instead of progressing, mistaking busyness for true productivity. In this chapter, we will explore how to uncover the blindspots in your current prioritization methods, enabling you to transform your professional life with purpose and intention. Understanding your blindspots is the first step toward making meaningful progress.

Let's dive into the often-hidden pitfalls and see where your priorities may be leading you astray, and, more importantly, how you can get back on track to achieve your career aspirations.

Assessing Your Current Prioritization Methods

The first step in unmasking priority blindspots is taking a hard look at how you're currently prioritizing your workload. Most professionals use some form of prioritization—whether it's a to-do list, a calendar, or even an instinctive sense of urgency—but these approaches are often flawed. What might feel like good prioritization could actually be a set of habits that keep you busy without moving you any closer to your big goals. It's time to assess these habits and question whether they are genuinely serving your growth.

Many of us have been conditioned to believe that if we can cross things off a list, we are being productive. Yet, productivity is not about getting more things done; it's about getting the right things done. This means some tasks on your daily agenda might need to go, no matter how satisfying they are to check off. The key is evaluating the efficiency of your existing methods. Ask yourself—is the system you're using actually leading you to your long-term aspirations, or is it simply keeping you afloat?

Take a moment to examine your current workflow. Do you prioritize based on urgency alone, or do you also consider the importance and long-term impact of each task? Do you end up spending hours on minor tasks that have no lasting impact, simply because they feel urgent? By honestly examining how you make decisions about your time, you'll start to see the cracks in your methods and find opportunities for improvement. For example, you might realize that you're prioritizing tasks that are easy to complete but offer little in terms of real progress. It's not just about getting things done—it's about getting the right things done, and that requires a deliberate shift in how you view prioritization. It's about adopting a mindset shift—seeing prioritization not as a chore, but as a strategy for career-defining success, where each decision about how you spend your time brings you closer to your goals.

Common Pitfalls in Professional Goal-Setting

When we talk about priorities, we have to talk about goal-setting—because it's our goals that ultimately shape what we choose to prioritize. But many people make mistakes here, often without realizing it. One of the biggest pitfalls is setting vague or broad goals. We all have aspirations like "be more successful" or "improve productivity," but these goals aren't actionable. They lack clarity, making it hard to map out the priorities that could get you there.

Another common pitfall is focusing on the wrong metrics. For instance, many people set goals that are focused on input rather than output—like spending more hours at work instead of aiming for a specific project outcome. The problem is that input-focused goals often miss the bigger picture. You could be clocking in long hours without making a real dent in what actually matters for your career progression.

Think about your current professional goals—are they clear and specific? Are they tied to outcomes that genuinely matter to your future success? It's easy to get caught up in goals that look good on paper but don't have any meaningful impact. You might find yourself pursuing goals that are impressive to others but don't truly satisfy your inner purpose. Perhaps you're chasing a promotion that doesn't align with your long-term vision, or you're committing to projects simply because they're available, not because they move you towards your true aspirations. Sometimes, we also set goals that reflect external pressures rather than our internal values, leading to a disconnect between our daily actions and what we truly want to achieve. It's important to recognize if your goals are fulfilling societal expectations rather than personal fulfillment. Only by identifying and correcting these misalignments can you ensure that the goals you set today will contribute to the future you genuinely desire.

The path to better goal-setting starts with clarity. You need to define what success looks like for you—not for your company, not for your colleagues, but for you. Only when you have that clarity can you start aligning your daily actions with your long-term aspirations.

Aligning Daily Actions with Long-Term Aspirations

Now that we've covered the common pitfalls, let's explore how to correct course. The key to making sure your priorities are truly serving your goals is alignment—the process of connecting your daily actions to your long-term aspirations. Too often, professionals drift through their days focusing on immediate fires, with no thought given to how those actions stack up towards a bigger picture. It's like spending all your time bailing water out of a sinking boat without patching the hole.

A practical way to align your actions is to start every day by reviewing your long-term goals. What are the top three to five achievements you want to reach this year? Write them down where you can see them daily. This exercise will serve as a compass for your short-term activities. When new tasks and opportunities come up, evaluate them against these big goals. Ask yourself: **Does this task move me toward my primary goals, or is it simply noise?**

To connect actions with aspirations, consider using a system like time-blocking. Allocate chunks of your schedule to work solely on what matters most to your long-term goals. By designating uninterrupted periods for your highest priorities, you ensure that your most crucial work gets done without interference. This practice not only boosts productivity but also cultivates a sense of focus and purpose that is often lacking when we allow ourselves to be distracted by lesser tasks. This prevents the "tyranny of the urgent"—when less important but time-sensitive tasks end up ruling your day, ultimately diverting energy and attention away from more meaningful projects. Protecting these blocks of time can dramatically increase the alignment between what you do and where you want to go, providing a consistent rhythm that helps you stay on track with your larger goals. It also serves as a reminder of your commitment to yourself and your future aspirations, reinforcing the idea that what truly matters deserves your best time and attention.

Remember, aligning your actions with your aspirations doesn't just mean working harder; it means working smarter. This might involve saying no to opportunities that do not serve your big-picture goals, which can be difficult at first. But every time you do, you're reclaiming your focus and directing it toward something that matters. And ultimately, this is how breakthroughs happen—not by doing more but by doing what matters.

Evaluate the Effectiveness of Current Prioritization Strategies

To truly unmask your priority blindspots, a final and essential step is to evaluate your current strategies honestly. Reflect on what has worked well and what hasn't over the past several months or years. Have you consistently felt fulfilled by the work you prioritize, or do you feel there are always important things left undone? Assessing effectiveness is crucial for fine-tuning your approach.

A helpful method here is the "Pareto Analysis," also known as the 80/20 Rule. The idea is simple—80% of your results come from 20% of your efforts. Look at your to-do list and identify which tasks or types of activities consistently lead to significant outcomes. Then, try to focus more of your time and energy on these high-impact activities, while cutting down on the less impactful ones.

You could also consider feedback from mentors, colleagues, or even your own reflections in a work journal. It's easy to think you're prioritizing effectively when you're busy. However, external input can reveal discrepancies between your perception of progress and actual, tangible outcomes. These insights will help you adjust your strategy so that your time and energy are invested in actions that genuinely move you forward.

In evaluating your strategies, you'll likely come across habits that need changing. Habits are powerful—they can either work in your favor or drag you down. The good news is that even small adjustments to your prioritization habits can create significant changes in the long run. By consistently choosing to focus on what matters most and letting go of the less important, you can transform your productivity, fulfillment, and overall career trajectory.

The Power of Saying No

One major hurdle when improving prioritization is the fear of saying no. It's natural to want to be helpful, to take on challenges, and to not disappoint others. But to prioritize effectively, you have to master the art of saying no—even to good opportunities—so that you have the space for the best opportunities. The truth is, saying yes to everything dilutes your focus, weakens your potential, and keeps you from making meaningful progress on what really matters.

The power of saying no lies in its ability to create room for true breakthroughs. Every time you say no to something less important, you're saying yes to something that aligns with your long-term aspirations. Start small—the next time you're offered a project or task that doesn't truly excite you or fit with your goals, politely decline. Use this newfound time to focus on the high-impact activities that are more deserving of your attention.

Saying no can be uncomfortable at first, especially in a professional setting where expectations are high, and opportunities might feel scarce. However, if you are clear about your priorities and can communicate that effectively, saying no becomes easier. Remember, people respect those who value their time and have a clear vision of their purpose. When you prioritize with confidence, others notice, and it often leads to higher quality work, better opportunities, and ultimately, greater success.

Using a Personal Inventory to Reveal Blindspots

To unmask your priority blindspots effectively, consider conducting a personal inventory of all your ongoing tasks and responsibilities. This exercise isn't meant to overwhelm but to bring clarity to everything you have on your plate. Write down every professional commitment, every side project, and even the personal to-dos that affect your energy and focus at work.

Once you have your inventory, classify each item into one of three categories:

1. **Essential for Career Growth**: Tasks that directly impact your long-term goals and aspirations.

2. **Necessary Maintenance**: Things that need to be done to keep you functioning effectively, but don't necessarily propel you forward.

3. **Non-Essential**: Activities that don't contribute meaningfully to your success or satisfaction.

This exercise can be eye-opening. Many professionals are surprised to find how much of their time is devoted to non-essential activities—those that do not move them closer to career breakthroughs but merely fill their schedules. By categorizing your responsibilities, you'll gain a clearer picture of what truly deserves your time and attention, and where you need to make adjustments.

Next - The Breakthrough Blocker Revolution

Having uncovered your blindspots and reevaluated your current prioritization methods, it's time to explore the revolutionary strategy that will propel you forward. In the next chapter, we introduce the Breakthrough Blocker Method, a practical framework that will help you use selective ignorance to transform your career and achieve extraordinary success.

"It is not enough to be busy.
The question is: What are we busy about?"
– Henry David Thoreau

Chapter Four

The Breakthrough Blocker Revolution

Selective ignorance can be your most powerful ally in achieving extraordinary success.

For most of us, the very idea of ignoring tasks is unnerving. We've been taught that success comes from relentless hard work, ticking off every item on our to-do list, and always being "on." But what if that narrative was all wrong? In this chapter, we're going to unravel why knowing what **not** to do is just as critical as knowing what to do. This revolutionary idea isn't about laziness—it's about focus, intent, and choosing your battles wisely. By embracing selective ignorance, you'll gain clarity and the freedom to drive your energy into what genuinely matters. Ultimately, selective ignorance is a strategy, not a shortcut, that will help you achieve professional breakthroughs that others can only dream of.

Letting go of low-impact, high-distraction activities is the first step toward unlocking your true potential.

Introduction to the Breakthrough Blocker Method

In a world that glorifies busyness, the Breakthrough Blocker Method is a radical shift toward true productivity.

The Breakthrough Blocker Method turns the conventional idea of success on its head. Instead of pushing you to cram your schedule with more tasks, this method asks: What should you ignore? It's about identifying the true barriers to your progress—the overwhelming volume of minor tasks, responsibilities, and distractions that keep you spinning your wheels without real movement forward. High-achievers often struggle with this the most because they're inclined to think they can "do it all." This mindset, though admirable, is often their biggest enemy.

The Breakthrough Blocker Method helps you consciously filter out the unimportant to create space for the impactful. The idea is simple but powerful: by blocking out the noise, you can focus on the signals that truly drive success. Imagine it as carving a statue from a solid block of marble—you have to eliminate what doesn't belong to reveal the masterpiece underneath. This method isn't about managing time; it's about managing attention and energy. It's a call to action for anyone who wants to move beyond feeling perpetually busy and finally start achieving significant breakthroughs.

By the end of this chapter, you'll have a clear understanding of why ignoring the right things can be one of the most strategic decisions you make.

How Selective Ignorance Fuels Extraordinary Success

Mastering selective ignorance isn't about neglect—it's about choosing purposefully where to invest your mental energy.

Most of us fall into the trap of thinking that every task on our list is equally important. We end up overcommitting, overworking, and overwhelming ourselves. What many don't realize is that **not all work is created equal**. Extraordinary success often requires you to make difficult choices about what deserves your attention and, more importantly, what doesn't. This is where selective ignorance comes in.

The principle behind selective ignorance is that, in a world where information and tasks are endless, the key to doing something remarkable lies in the **ruthless prioritization** of your focus. Think of it like a magnifying glass—by concentrating sunlight into one sharp beam, you can start a fire. Spread that same light across a broader area, and it's merely warmth. Focusing intensely on fewer things allows you to produce an outsized impact compared to spreading your energy too thin.

Bill Gates, Warren Buffett, and Steve Jobs were famous for their ability to zero in on what mattered and dismiss what didn't. They weren't afraid to ignore non-essential tasks, meetings, and even entire projects because they understood that selective ignorance is a crucial ingredient of sustained success. These examples highlight that extraordinary achievements require something far beyond time management. It takes courage to ignore the noise—to cut out the excess so that only the essential remains. And therein lies the secret: *what you choose not to do defines your success just as much as what you choose to do.*

Selective ignorance fuels success by giving you back the mental bandwidth needed to solve challenging problems and innovate.

Setting the Stage for Your 30-Day Transformation

Your journey with the Breakthrough Blocker Method starts with a commitment to clarity and ruthless prioritization.

This 30-day transformation is about **unlearning** much of what you've been taught about productivity. It's about building a foundation where the goal isn't to be perpetually busy but to focus on what truly matters for your breakthrough. Over the next month, you'll be guided through exercises that help you identify your key blockers, eliminate distractions, and align your efforts with your core objectives.

The transformation begins with a diagnostic phase—getting brutally honest about where your time goes. You'll create a list of everything that's demanding your attention. This inventory will help you recognize patterns, spot productivity black holes, and start categorizing your tasks in a way that brings clarity. Once this is done, the next step is to implement the Breakthrough Blocker Test—a litmus test for determining whether each activity on your list is worth your time or whether it should be ignored.

The next 30 days will be about practicing selective ignorance deliberately. The Breakthrough Blocker Method isn't just a tactic—it's a mindset that requires constant, conscious effort. Every day, you will be making choices about what tasks get your focus and what tasks you choose to ignore, knowing that every "no" creates more room for impactful "yeses."

By committing to this 30-day transformation, you're preparing yourself for a shift in how you operate, think, and approach your work.

The Breakthrough Blocker Test: How to Determine What to Ignore

One of the most critical elements of the Breakthrough Blocker Method is the Breakthrough Blocker Test.

The Breakthrough Blocker Test is a simple yet powerful question: "**Does this directly contribute to my long-term goals or current breakthrough objective?**" If the answer is no, it's a blocker that needs to be ignored. Often, the challenge isn't that we don't know what our priorities are—it's that we get distracted by a constant influx of small, seemingly urgent demands that pull us away from meaningful work.

Using the Breakthrough Blocker Test daily will help you categorize tasks based on their importance and direct relevance to your goals. Here's how to apply the test effectively:

1. **List All Current Tasks**: Begin by writing down every task that you need to do. Don't filter anything out; get it all on paper.

2. **Ask the Key Question**: For each task, ask: "Does this directly contribute to my long-term goals or current breakthrough objective?"

3. **Categorize**: If the task passes the test, mark it as **essential**. If it doesn't, mark it as a **blocker** that should be ignored or delegated.

This isn't an easy process. Often, you'll feel the impulse to do things because they seem immediately important or because you're afraid of the consequences of not doing them. But selective ignorance requires you to trust that by saying "no" to low-impact activities, you're creating room for significant, focused progress.

Over time, applying the Breakthrough Blocker Test will become second nature, and you'll be amazed at how much more effective and impactful your work becomes.

Strategies for Overcoming Guilt and Anxiety Associated with Ignoring Tasks

One of the biggest barriers to embracing selective ignorance is the guilt associated with saying "no."

For many, ignoring tasks feels uncomfortable, as if they're being irresponsible or letting someone down. This guilt is amplified by cultural norms that glorify constant busyness and productivity as a measure of worth. To truly succeed with the Breakthrough Blocker Method, it's crucial to learn how to overcome these feelings of guilt and anxiety.

First, **reframe your perspective**. Saying "no" isn't about shirking responsibilities; it's about ensuring that your time is devoted to what matters most. Understand that every time you say "yes" to something trivial, you're saying "no" to something significant. To help with this, it may be useful to visualize your time and energy as limited resources. Imagine your focus as a cup of water. If you keep pouring it into a dozen different cups, none of them will ever fill. However, if you pour it into just one or two cups, they overflow.

Another strategy is to **replace guilt with purpose**. Every time you decide not to do something, remind yourself why. Reconnect with your breakthrough objective—what are you ultimately working toward? What is the big-picture success that will make the small sacrifices worth it? This sense of purpose can help override the immediate discomfort of saying "no" to tasks.

Lastly, **communicate clearly**. When you choose to ignore or delegate tasks, make sure the people involved understand why. Often, guilt comes from fear of others' judgments. By explaining that you're focusing on high-impact work that benefits everyone in the long run, you can alleviate some of this pressure and help others see the bigger picture.

Embracing selective ignorance is as much an emotional challenge as it is a strategic one—but once you learn to overcome these internal barriers, you'll be on your way to extraordinary success.

Why Saying "No" is the Ultimate Productivity Hack

Productivity isn't about doing more; it's about doing what matters most—and sometimes that means doing **nothing** at all.

The power of "no" can be transformative. By deliberately choosing not to do something, you protect your focus, energy, and time. This means saying "no" not only to tasks that don't align with your goals but also to distractions, unnecessary meetings, and even certain opportunities that don't serve your long-term objectives. The reality is, every "yes" has an opportunity cost—saying "yes" to one thing means saying "no" to another, often more important, thing. Understanding this trade-off is key to mastering the Breakthrough Blocker Method.

High-performers understand this principle deeply. They know that their success depends not on how much they do but on what they choose not to do. By being selective, they channel their energies into fewer activities that yield disproportionately high returns. They recognize that spreading their attention across countless tasks leads to mediocrity, whereas focusing on a select few allows them to achieve excellence. To do this effectively, you must develop an awareness of your goals, understand what truly drives your progress, and cultivate the discipline to defend your time against the endless demands of modern work life. This means setting boundaries, communicating them effectively, and being comfortable with the discomfort of letting go of the less important tasks.

A practical approach to implementing "no" in your life is to **create a "not-to-do" list** alongside your daily task list. This list should include activities that are often time-consuming but low value, like unproductive meetings, excessive email responses, or tasks that could be delegated. Keeping these activities visible serves as a constant reminder of what you need to avoid in order to maintain focus on what truly matters.

Saying "no" isn't easy, but it is the ultimate productivity hack—the difference between those who achieve extraordinary results and those who are perpetually busy but stuck in mediocrity.

Finding Hidden Patterns...

Now that you've grasped the power of selective ignorance, it's time to dive deeper into how you can map out your professional landscape in Chapter 5. You'll learn how to categorize your tasks and projects, identify hidden patterns, and start building a clearer picture of where your focus needs to go. This is the next crucial step on your path to achieving breakthrough success.

"Do less, be more."
– Elizabeth Grace Saunders
(Time management coach and author)

Chapter Five

The CLEAR Path to Breakthrough

The CLEAR framework is the blueprint for transforming overwhelm into success.

In this chapter, we're stepping into a new era of prioritization. It's not just about doing more or working harder; it's about doing what matters most. The CLEAR framework is your structured pathway to unlock focus, prioritize effectively, and truly make progress in areas that count. It brings clarity to what often feels chaotic, enabling you to move beyond the noise and zero in on career-defining opportunities. In this chapter, you'll learn not only what CLEAR stands for but also how to make it an indispensable part of your journey towards breakthroughs.

The CLEAR method isn't just another productivity hack—it's a foundational strategy that changes how you approach every task, project, and decision. Each element of the CLEAR acronym will come to life here: from organizing tasks to eliminating non-essentials, this is where we start transforming ideas into action. By the end of this chapter, you'll not only understand what CLEAR is but also feel equipped and inspired to use it in real, impactful ways.

Imagine no longer feeling overwhelmed but instead moving forward with clear, deliberate purpose.

Overview of the Breakthrough Blocker Method Framework: CLEAR

How would your life change if you knew exactly where to focus every day? For many, the overwhelm of juggling tasks and responsibilities makes it hard to see the way forward. The CLEAR framework is designed to shift that experience. **CLEAR** is an acronym that stands for **Categorize, List, Eliminate, Act, Refine** — five actionable steps that will help you prioritize effectively, cut out distractions, and focus on tasks that bring true breakthroughs.

The Breakthrough Blocker Method, powered by CLEAR, isn't about piling on more to your already long to-do list. Instead, it's about achieving **depth instead of breadth**. It helps to clearly categorize tasks, prioritize what really matters, strategically ignore what doesn't, and continuously refine your approach for even more success.

This chapter will guide you through each part of CLEAR, setting you up to tackle overwhelm by giving you a method to create order from chaos. With this structure in place, you can achieve a focused state of mind where every action feels intentional and impactful.

The Science Behind Effective Prioritization and Focused Action

Multitasking might feel productive, but it's often a trap that leads to inefficiency. Research has shown that focusing on fewer tasks results in higher quality work and faster completion times. Our brains aren't designed to switch constantly between unrelated activities. Each time we do, we waste valuable mental energy in the transition. Studies by neuroscientists have demonstrated that the more we switch between tasks, the more our productivity declines.

With the CLEAR framework, the aim is to leverage **focused action**. This means dedicating your energy to fewer, more impactful tasks. Consider the work of the world's most successful people—they're not successful because they do everything, but because they focus on doing the right things exceptionally well. A big part of this success is understanding the importance of **deep work**. This is a concept introduced by Cal Newport, which highlights that the ability to focus on complex tasks without distraction is becoming increasingly rare and valuable.

By focusing on meaningful tasks rather than spreading your energy thin, you move closer to breakthroughs. Prioritization is not just about managing your time better; it's about taking control of where your energy goes. This chapter explores why focused, deliberate action makes all the difference. We'll also talk about the psychological effects of reducing your workload by letting go of unnecessary tasks—a powerful move that enhances productivity and well-being.

Preparing for Your Personalized Breakthrough Journey

Transforming how you work, starts with small, deliberate changes. Before diving into each component of CLEAR, it's important to prepare yourself mentally and practically. This step is about ensuring you're ready to start making decisions differently, to cut out the noise, and focus on what's meaningful.

- **Mindset Shifts**: Embrace the idea that doing less can actually mean accomplishing more. Many of us have been conditioned to equate productivity with busyness. However, this chapter will help you break free from that mindset by showing you the power of focusing on fewer, high-impact activities.

- **Organize Your Tasks**: Start by listing every task you currently have on your plate. Don't filter; write it all down, even the things you've been meaning to do but haven't gotten to yet. The idea here is to have a complete inventory of what's competing for your attention. This task inventory is your starting point for the categorization step of the CLEAR process. You can reference back to Chapter 2 – Mapping Your Mental Clutter -where you made a list of all you have on your plate. You can review your list, and if you missed anything, you can add to the list, to use it here.

- **Set Expectations**: Understand that adopting the CLEAR framework is a process. It's not about flipping a switch overnight—it's about making incremental changes that lead to long-term breakthroughs. This journey is about building habits and mindsets that ensure you stay focused on what truly matters.

Preparing for your breakthrough journey involves more than just organizing your tasks—it's about creating space in your life for strategic action. By starting with a fresh mindset and a clear understanding of what's currently consuming your time, you'll be ready to make the decisions that drive your biggest career breakthroughs.

Categorize: Mapping Your Professional Landscape

To focus on what matters, you first need to understand everything that demands your attention. The categorization phase of the CLEAR framework is about mapping out your professional landscape. What does your workload really look like, and where are your efforts currently going? This is where the full list of your tasks—both big and small—gets organized into distinct categories.

1. **Categorize by Value**: Every task falls into one of three categories: High Value, Medium Value, or Low Value. High Value tasks are those that contribute significantly to your career breakthroughs. Medium Value tasks are necessary, but they do not lead directly to major growth. Low Value tasks are the time-wasters—these are often dis-

tractions that feel productive but actually keep you from meaningful work.

1. **Categorize by Urgency**: Many tasks feel urgent, but they're not all equally important. Understanding which of your tasks are truly urgent and which ones are falsely urgent helps you allocate time effectively. This is where the distinction between **urgent versus important** becomes crucial—a concept Stephen Covey highlighted in his famous time management matrix.

Categorizing tasks brings **clarity to chaos**. When you know exactly which tasks matter most, you're ready to move forward with clear priorities. During this stage, don't worry about eliminating anything yet—your goal is simply to understand the landscape clearly and objectively.

List Priorities: Defining Your North Star

Defining your priorities is like finding your North Star—it keeps you on track. Once you've categorized your tasks, the next step is to list your top priorities. This isn't just about picking what's most important in the moment—it's about aligning your actions with your long-term goals.

- **Identify True Priorities**: Ask yourself, "If I could only accomplish three things this week, what would they be?" This forces you to get real about what matters most. Your goal is to identify a handful of tasks that, if completed, will move the needle significantly in your career or life.

- **Rank Your Priorities**: Once you have your top priorities, rank them in order of importance. Be ruthless about what you put at the top—you're aiming for focus, not volume. This list will serve as a filter for deciding what to work on at any given moment.

- **Align with Long-Term Goals**: Each task on your priority list should have a clear connection to your long-term aspirations. The tasks that make it onto this list aren't just urgent or necessary—they're instrumental to your broader success.

Creating a list of priorities gives you the clarity needed to take focused action. **Your priorities are your North Star**—they guide you through each day, ensuring you stay aligned with what truly matters. This focus is the key to turning daily efforts into significant, career-defining outcomes.

Eliminate: Mastering the Art of Strategic Ignorance

You can't do everything, and that's perfectly okay. The elimination phase of the CLEAR framework is all about strategically ignoring tasks that don't serve your highest goals. This is where you take your task inventory and begin eliminating anything that isn't high-impact.

1. **The Breakthrough Blocker Test**: A simple but powerful question to ask yourself when deciding whether to keep or cut a task is: "Does this help me achieve my breakthrough goal?" If the answer is no, it's time to let it go. Many tasks feel necessary simply because they've always been there, but this doesn't mean they are contributing to your success.

2. **Overcoming Guilt**: One of the biggest challenges with elimination is emotional. People often feel guilty for saying no—whether it's turning down a meeting, ignoring an email, or deciding not to finish an old project. But consider this: **each 'yes' to a low-value task is a 'no' to a high-impact opportunity**. Eliminating the non-essential is how you create the space necessary for growth.

3. **Tackle Time-Wasters**: Review your low-value tasks and start eliminating. Perhaps there's a regular meeting that's more of a status update than a decision-making session—propose moving it to an email instead. The key here is to **protect your energy and time** for the things that genuinely matter.

Strategic elimination isn't about cutting corners; it's about protecting your time so you can focus on what truly counts. By eliminating tasks that don't serve your breakthrough goals, you give yourself the freedom and space to pursue those that do.

Act: From Decision to Breakthrough

Once you know what to do, it's time to act. This stage of the CLEAR framework is all about moving from intention to action—from knowing your priorities to doing them. Action is what ultimately differentiates dreams from reality.

- **Focused Work Sessions**: Set aside dedicated blocks of time to work on your high-priority tasks. These focused work sessions should be free from interruptions and distractions. Use techniques like **Pomodoro** or **time-blocking** to ensure you stay on track.

- **Overcoming Resistance**: Many people struggle to take action because of procrastination or fear. Understand that resistance is normal; it's a sign that what you're about to do is meaningful. One way to combat resistance is to break a task into smaller steps. Focus on starting rather than finishing—often, getting started is the hardest part.

- **Track Your Progress**: Progress isn't always obvious. By tracking what you accomplish each day, you maintain motivation and ensure you're moving toward your breakthrough goal. Whether you use a journal or a digital tool, make it a habit to acknowledge what you've achieved.

Action bridges the gap between where you are and where you want to be. The CLEAR framework isn't just about understanding what to do—it's about creating an environment where action is natural and consistent. Every focused work session is a step towards your ultimate breakthrough.

Refine: Evolving Your Breakthrough Strategy

No plan is perfect from the start—refinement is essential to long-term success. The final step in the CLEAR framework is about reviewing your progress and making adjustments as needed. As you put your plan into action, you'll discover what works well and where you might need to pivot.

- **Continuous Improvement**: Set aside time each week to review your progress. Ask yourself: What went well? What could I improve? These reflection sessions are where you learn and adapt. The idea isn't to be perfect but to get better over time.

- **Adaptation**: Life changes, and so do priorities. Perhaps a new opportunity arises, or your career goals shift. The refinement step gives you the flexibility to adjust the CLEAR framework to fit your current situation. This adaptability ensures the framework stays relevant, no matter what life throws at you.

- **Recommit to Your North Star**: Refinement isn't just about changing what doesn't work; it's also about recommitting to what does. Every week, reaffirm your top priorities and decide what you'll focus on. This regular recommitment keeps you aligned and motivated.

Refining your approach ensures that your journey isn't stagnant. **Growth requires evolution**. The CLEAR framework isn't a static plan—it's a living process that evolves with you, helping you stay on course and continue progressing toward your breakthroughs.

Moving Forward with Clarity and Confidence

The CLEAR framework gives you a powerful tool to navigate the chaos of modern work and life. It's not just a method; it's a mindset that prioritizes depth over breadth, intentionality over busyness, and meaningful action over mere activity. By categorizing tasks, defining priorities, eliminating distractions, taking focused action, and refining your approach, you have everything you need to make genuine progress toward your goals.

With each element of the CLEAR framework, you're moving away from the overwhelm that holds so many back and towards a state of focus that drives real success. This is about creating breakthroughs that aren't just fleeting wins but lasting, career-defining achievements. The process may not be without its challenges—you'll face resistance, difficult decisions, and times when you must adjust your path—but with the CLEAR framework, you have a guide that ensures your efforts are meaningful and impactful.

Gaining a New Level of Clarity...

As we move into the next chapter, we'll start diving deeper into how to categorize and manage the complexities of your professional landscape effectively. You'll learn the specific techniques that will help you fully map out your commitments and understand which tasks demand your focus. Get ready to gain a new level of clarity that will serve as the foundation for all the breakthroughs to come.

"The successful warrior is the average man, with laser-like focus."
– Bruce Lee

Chapter Six

Categorize: Mapping Your Professional Landscape

The ability to categorize tasks effectively is the cornerstone of personal productivity.

In today's high-speed professional environment, we often find ourselves juggling countless tasks, projects, and expectations. The sheer number of responsibilities can make it difficult to see the forest for the trees. Without a structured approach to organizing these commitments, even the most talented professionals can feel overwhelmed and lose sight of what truly matters. In this chapter, we take a closer look at how categorizing your tasks and projects can help you gain clarity, regain control, and set yourself up for significant breakthroughs.

The art of categorization is about more than simply making lists—it's about understanding your workload from a strategic perspective, revealing hidden patterns, and focusing on what drives real progress. By mapping your professional landscape, you will be equipped to identify areas of unnecessary effort, opportunities for delegation, and the activities that bring the highest value. This chapter will introduce a straightforward yet powerful approach to task categorization that will transform how you view and manage your professional life.

The following pages will provide the tools you need to inventory your commitments comprehensively, break them down into meaningful categories, and unearth the patterns that shape your productivity. This process is not just about getting organized—it's about laying the foundation for making smarter decisions, prioritizing effectively, and ultimately taking control of your path to career success.

Techniques for Effective Task and Project Categorization

Your productivity starts with understanding the categories of work you engage with every day. One of the simplest yet most powerful strategies you can employ is dividing your tasks into a set of clear, actionable categories. Many professionals default to broad categories such as "work," "home," and "personal," but in the context of creating breakthroughs, you need more refined distinctions. Let's delve into the process of categorizing effectively to give you a sharper lens on your commitments.

1. **Define Action-Based Categories**

    - Start by defining categories based on the nature of the actions they require. Examples include "Decision-Making Tasks," "Collaborative Projects," "Administrative Duties," and "Creative Work." Decision-Making Tasks might include activities such as evaluating strategic options, prioritizing projects, and making key business decisions that significantly impact outcomes. These tasks require intense focus and critical thinking, often best approached during your peak mental hours. Collaborative Projects involve working alongside colleagues to develop ideas, solve problems, or create joint deliverables. Effective collaboration demands communication, teamwork, and adaptability, which means these tasks are best scheduled when others are available and when your energy allows for constructive interaction. Administrative Duties consist of routine yet necessary activities, such as organizing schedules, managing emails, or updating documentation. These tasks, while often repetitive, are crucial to maintaining operational flow and can usually be tackled during times of lower mental energy. Lastly, Creative Work encompasses activities like brainstorming, designing, writing, or developing innovative solutions. Such tasks thrive on inspiration and mental clarity, making it essential to identify when you are most creatively energized. Each category should reflect the type of mental energy and resources needed, allowing you to structure your day more deliberately, ensuring that you are working on the right types of tasks at the optimal times for maximum productivity and impact.

2. **The Importance vs. Urgency Matrix**
   - The **Eisenhower Matrix**, popularized by Stephen Covey, remains a powerful tool for categorization. Classify your tasks based on two factors: importance and urgency. Tasks that are both important and urgent go to the top of your list, while those that are neither should be considered for elimination or deferred. Tasks that are important but not urgent should be scheduled for focused work sessions to ensure they receive adequate attention, whereas tasks that are urgent but not important should ideally be delegated to free up your time. This approach not only helps in managing immediate responsibilities but also in allocating time for long-term, strategic goals. This exercise helps highlight what truly drives progress in your career, enabling you to take control of your daily activities and align them more effectively with your overarching objectives.
3. **Energy Mapping**
   - Not all tasks require the same amount of mental energy. By categorizing tasks according to the type of energy they require—be it analytical, creative, or in-

terpersonal—you can align them with your energy levels throughout the day. Analytical tasks, such as data analysis or strategic planning, demand intense focus and logical thinking, making them suitable for times when your mind is sharpest. Creative work, like writing, designing, or brainstorming, benefits most from peak mental energy, often during early mornings or other times of high clarity. Interpersonal tasks, including meetings, networking, or collaborative discussions, need emotional and social energy, which is often best during mid-day when you can be at your most engaging. By categorizing in this way, you can better match tasks to the natural ebbs and flows of your mental energy throughout the day. For instance, creative work may be best tackled during your peak focus hours, while administrative duties such as responding to emails or organizing files could be scheduled for times when your energy naturally dips. This strategic alignment ensures that you are operating at maximum efficiency and prevents burnout by balancing high-energy and low-energy activities effectively.

4. **Outcome-Based Categorization**

    - Group tasks according to the outcomes they lead to. This approach keeps you focused on results rather than activities, ensuring that every action you take is driving tangible progress. Begin by identifying the key outcomes that are most important for your career trajectory. For example, categorize tasks that contribute to different career objectives—such as skill development, strategic projects, revenue generation, process optimization, and networking. Skill development could involve activities like taking courses, reading relevant literature, or practicing specific skills, all of which lead to personal and professional growth. Strategic projects might include initiatives that push your career forward, such as leading a new program or spearheading a critical business initiative. Revenue-generating tasks, on the other hand, include activities directly related to driving sales or closing deals, which are crucial for business growth. Process optimization might involve refining workflows or developing new systems to increase efficiency, whereas networking encompasses all actions taken to grow your professional network, like attending industry events, following up with contacts, or engaging in online forums. This makes it easier to see which actions align directly with your long-term goals and helps to ensure that your time is being invested in efforts that generate significant career advancements and personal achievements.

By breaking your work down into these focused categories, you begin to create a roadmap for understanding and managing your commitments in a much more strategic manner. This process not only helps you allocate time effectively but also makes it easier to identify which commitments are holding you back from making a real impact.

Creating a Comprehensive Inventory of Your Professional Commitments

To gain control, you first need to know what you're dealing with. It may seem tedious, but creating a comprehensive inventory of all your professional tasks and commitments is a vital first step. This inventory provides a clear, unfiltered look at everything that is currently on your plate, offering insights that could reveal the reason behind your stress or the factors affecting your productivity.

1. **Audit Your To-Dos**
    - Begin by auditing all the tasks you're currently responsible for—both big and small. It helps to make this list exhaustive and detailed, capturing everything from major project milestones to routine activities such as checking emails. You'd be surprised how often seemingly minor tasks pile up and create major burdens.
2. **List Projects and Recurring Tasks**
    - Differentiate between tasks that are one-off and those that are part of ongoing projects. Recurring responsibilities, like weekly meetings or monthly reports, often slip under the radar because they're routine. These

recurring commitments can take up significant time and energy, so capturing them explicitly is key to understanding your true workload.

1. **Assess Time and Effort**
   - Once you've created a comprehensive list, it's essential to estimate the time and effort each item requires. This process will help you gauge where most of your time is being allocated. You might discover that low-value tasks are consuming an outsized share of your time, offering a clear target for elimination or delegation.
2. **Identify Dependencies**
   - It's also helpful to mark tasks that depend on other people or factors outside your control. Recognizing these dependencies will give you insights into potential bottlenecks and help you understand what's within your power to change and what's not.

This inventory is your baseline—it's the comprehensive map of your professional terrain. Only with this clarity can you begin to categorize, prioritize, and ultimately eliminate what's standing in your way.

Identifying Hidden Patterns in Your Workload

Identifying patterns within your commitments is crucial for making informed decisions. By categorizing tasks and creating an inventory, you've gathered data about where your time and energy go. Now, it's time to dig deeper and reveal the hidden patterns that are either hindering or enhancing your productivity.

1. **Spotting Redundant Activities**
   - Look for tasks that you end up doing repeatedly with minimal impact. These redundant activities can easily drain energy without contributing to your broader goals. Identifying these is the first step toward streamlining or even eliminating unnecessary processes. For example, can you automate routine email responses or delegate meeting preparations to a colleague?
2. **Recognizing High-Value Actions**
   - On the flip side, identify tasks that provide outsized returns relative to the effort they require. These are your "breakthrough actions"—the ones that lead to significant progress in your career or open up new opportunities. By categorizing these actions separately, you can see where you need to allocate more of your time.

1. **Balancing Reactive vs. Proactive Work**

    - Many professionals spend a disproportionate amount of time on reactive tasks—responding to emails, attending last-minute meetings, and putting out fires. Categorizing your work allows you to see just how much of your time is consumed by reactive versus proactive activities. The goal is to gradually shift towards more proactive work, where you drive your schedule instead of reacting to it.

2. **Identifying Bottlenecks**

    - If you've listed tasks with dependencies on other people, you're likely to find patterns of delay or inefficiency. For instance, if multiple tasks are waiting on the same person, it might indicate that this person's availability is a bottleneck for your progress. Recognizing these patterns lets you create contingency plans or adjust expectations, reducing stress and enhancing flow.

Identifying these patterns provides you with insights that allow you to make smarter decisions about what you should be focusing on and where you can cut back. Your workload is not just a series of tasks; it's a collection of habits and routines that shape your effectiveness.

Putting It All Together: A Clearer Professional Landscape

At this stage, you should now have a comprehensive map of your commitments and the hidden patterns within them. It's time to pull these insights together into a clear, organized picture of your professional landscape—a picture that helps you see exactly where you stand and what actions you need to take next.

1. **Visualize Your Task Map**
    - Consider using a visual aid to represent your commitments. You could create a mind map, a Gantt chart, or a simple grid that groups your tasks by category, priority, and urgency. Visual representations can often reveal relationships and patterns that a simple list cannot.
2. **Set Realistic Priorities**
    - With everything laid out, the next step is to decide on priorities. Be honest about what tasks truly matter and what can either wait or be delegated. You've already categorized based on importance, urgency, and energy—now it's about making the tough choices to focus your time on the things that will make the biggest difference.

1. **Communicate Boundaries**

    - Sometimes, gaining control means setting boundaries with others. Now that you have a clear understanding of your workload, communicate these boundaries with your colleagues or clients. Let them know what your priorities are and where your capacity lies. Doing so isn't about letting people down—it's about being realistic so you can contribute at your best.

2. **Use Insights for Future Planning**

    - Now that you've analyzed your commitments, categorized them, and set priorities, use this information to plan ahead. Don't let yourself slide back into reactive mode. Schedule regular check-ins with yourself—weekly, monthly, or quarterly—to reevaluate your workload and make sure that you're staying aligned with your larger career goals.

Categorizing your professional landscape isn't just an exercise in organization; it's a strategic move that lets you direct your efforts where they'll be most impactful. With your tasks mapped, prioritized, and categorized, you're in a position to start eliminating the distractions and time-wasters that have kept you from focusing on what really matters.

Defining Your North Star...

With a solid understanding of your professional landscape and a clear categorization of your tasks, it's time to move forward. In the next chapter, we'll dive into how to define your true priorities—your North Star—and ensure that your actions are directly aligned with your career breakthrough goals. You've mapped the terrain; now it's time to chart your path.

"Strive not to be a success, but rather to be of value."
- Albert Einstein

Chapter Seven

List Priorities: Defining Your North Star

Defining your true priorities is like setting a compass that guides every decision you make.

Without a clear sense of direction, many professionals get lost in the noise of endless tasks, feeling busy but making little real progress. This chapter will help you uncover, articulate, and align with your true priorities, your "North Star," allowing you to take actions that resonate with your highest goals.

Understanding what truly matters in your career is no small feat, especially when the pressure of immediate tasks can obscure what's important. You might be working tirelessly, but if your actions aren't aligned with what genuinely contributes to your long-term vision, you're just expending energy without progress. In this chapter, we'll dig into how you can identify which priorities truly deserve your time and energy, separating them from the distractions that can easily throw you off course.

By the end, you'll have a clear and actionable set of priorities that guide every choice, making each action count. This clarity will transform how you approach not only your workday but also how you define success for yourself, ensuring your actions are always pulling you closer to your aspirations.

Criteria for Identifying True Priorities

To figure out your real priorities, you need a system—something that makes it simple to distinguish what matters from what merely feels urgent. One effective tool is a **decision-making matrix**. This isn't just about plotting tasks in a chart, but rather about analyzing their true value in relation to your ultimate goals. Imagine a four-quadrant matrix: one axis represents the impact of the task, while the other represents its urgency.

- **High Impact, High Urgency**: These are tasks that need your immediate attention and genuinely contribute to your long-term success. They demand focus.
- **High Impact, Low Urgency**: This quadrant holds the tasks that are most often neglected. They aren't pressing, but their significance is unmatched—such as planning for future growth, skills development, or strategic thinking. This is the sweet spot where real breakthroughs happen.

- **Low Impact, High Urgency**: These are the tasks that often make you feel busy. Replying to every email, attending meetings with little significance—they feel important, but in reality, they're just keeping you spinning your wheels.

- **Low Impact, Low Urgency**: These are distractions, pure and simple. Eliminating or delegating these tasks should be your first move.

The matrix allows you to visualize and categorize your to-dos in a meaningful way. **The true art here lies in being honest with yourself** about what actually moves the needle versus what just keeps you preoccupied. We're often seduced by the allure of the urgent, even when it doesn't truly push us toward our goals. The aim here is to make strategic decisions about what deserves your attention.

Aligning Short-term Actions with Long-term Career Goals

Once you've established what your priorities are, the next step is to align your daily actions with those big, long-term career goals. Think of this as connecting the dots between where you are now and where you want to be. Without this connection, it's easy to find yourself busy with tasks that have little relevance to your ultimate vision.

A great starting point is to **visualize your long-term goal** in crystal-clear detail. Imagine exactly what you want to achieve in the next five or ten years—whether it's a leadership role, a certain lifestyle, or building an industry-changing product. Then work backwards: what does that look like a year from now? What does it look like six months from now? This kind of reverse-engineering helps break overwhelming, big dreams into manageable actions.

- **Map out Milestones**: Identify key milestones that signify progress towards your goal. These milestones act like checkpoints that allow you to assess whether your short-term efforts are taking you closer to or further away from your end goals.

- **Daily Impact Evaluation**: At the end of each day, evaluate how your activities contributed to these milestones. This can be as simple as a quick mental checklist or a reflective journal entry. Did you dedicate time to tasks in the "high impact, low urgency" quadrant? Or were you consumed by low-impact, urgent distractions?

Aligning your actions doesn't just keep you productive, it keeps you purposeful. It ensures that every small task or decision is a step towards a bigger picture. It makes each day count for something more significant than just getting through a to-do list.

Techniques for Resolving Conflicting Priorities

Conflicting priorities are inevitable. There will always be days when it feels like everything is screaming for your attention at once.

To handle this, you need a **set of strategies** to make the best possible decisions without getting overwhelmed.

One of the most effective strategies is to **use a value filter**. A value filter is essentially a question you ask yourself: *Does this action align with my highest values and goals?* If the answer is no, it's a clear signal that the task should be reconsidered—delegated, delayed, or eliminated altogether.

- **Negotiate When Necessary**: Sometimes conflicting priorities come from others—bosses, colleagues, or clients. Don't be afraid to negotiate timelines or expectations. Often, the people placing demands on you aren't fully aware of what else is on your plate. Politely communicating your current priorities and offering alternative solutions can prevent you from being overcommitted.

- **Set Clear Boundaries**: It's important to have boundaries around what is truly non-negotiable in your schedule. Blocking off uninterrupted time for deep work, for instance, is a boundary that ensures you stay focused on tasks that align with your true priorities.

- **Decision Fatigue Management**: On days when everything seems equally important, decision fatigue can creep in, making it difficult to choose what to tackle first. A helpful tool here is to **pre-decide** your priorities during weekly planning. Use a Sunday evening or Monday morning session to decide what your major focuses for the week will be—this way, you reduce the emotional drain of making in-the-moment decisions about what's most important.

Remember, conflicting priorities often cause stress because they make us feel like we're falling short somewhere. **But by actively filtering, negotiating, and setting boundaries, you give yourself the power to stay on course** with what truly matters. You'll find that not everything can or should be done—and that's perfectly okay.

Creating Your Personal Priority Map

To fully harness the power of prioritization, you need to create a **personal priority map**. This is a visual representation of where your efforts should be concentrated, allowing you to clearly see your most significant tasks and commitments.

- **Step 1: List Everything Out**: Write down every current project, task, and commitment you have. Don't hold back—include everything from work assignments to personal commitments. Again, you can reference previous lists you made in earlier chapters.

- **Step 2: Categorize According to Impact and Urgency**: Place each item in the decision-making matrix we discussed earlier. This process alone often brings a surprising amount of clarity.

- **Step 3: Focus on the High Impact Tasks**: Once everything is categorized, identify the high-impact items that align most closely with your long-term goals. These are the tasks that deserve the majority of your focus and energy.

The benefit of a priority map is that it gives you a **bird's-eye view** of what matters most. It shifts you away from reactive decision-making—where you respond based on what feels urgent—towards proactive planning that puts your career goals at the forefront.

The Cost of Misplaced Priorities

It's also worth discussing what happens when priorities are misplaced. When we confuse busyness for true progress, the cost can be significant. **Opportunities are missed**, relationships might suffer, and burnout becomes a real risk. Many ambitious professionals have found themselves stuck on a treadmill—moving fast but staying in the same place.

Misplaced priorities can lead to a sense of stagnation. You might feel busy all day long, but when you take a step back, it's hard to identify any meaningful progress. This feeling can be draining, slowly eroding your motivation and passion for your work. By intentionally mapping out priorities and staying aligned with your North Star, you can sidestep this trap entirely.

Establishing a Feedback Loop

A critical part of prioritization is to **establish a feedback loop** that keeps you on track. Priorities aren't set in stone; they can evolve as your career evolves. This is where the concept of **regular reflection and adjustment** comes in.

- **Weekly Reviews**: Set aside time each week to review your progress. Which tasks did you accomplish that pushed you closer to your goals? What unexpected challenges arose, and how did you handle them? This weekly review is an opportunity to celebrate small wins and recalibrate your focus for the upcoming week.

- **Monthly Check-ins**: On a broader scale, conduct a monthly check-in to assess how well your current priorities align with your long-term vision. Are the milestones you set still relevant, or has something changed in your career that requires you to adjust your direction?

Feedback loops aren't about finding faults—they're about ensuring alignment. They allow you to stay adaptable, ensuring that your actions always reflect what's most important.

Practical Steps for Immediate Implementation

To help you put all of this into action, let's break it down into **practical, immediately implementable steps**:

1. **Create Your Priority Matrix**: Dedicate an hour to categorizing your tasks into the four quadrants—impact versus urgency. This exercise alone can offer massive clarity.

1. **Define Your North Star**: Spend time defining what success looks like for you in five to ten years. The clearer your vision, the easier it will be to align your daily actions.

2. **Set Milestones**: Break down your long-term goals into smaller milestones. Each milestone becomes a target, giving your efforts a tangible outcome.

3. **Weekly Planning**: Start each week by identifying your top three priorities—tasks that align closely with your North Star. Focus your energy there.

4. **Establish Boundaries**: Decide on non-negotiable times for deep work. Communicate these to those around you, ensuring that these blocks remain protected.

Time to Start Eliminating Distractions...

Prioritization isn't about doing more; it's about doing what matters.

With a clear set of priorities guiding your actions, you're ready to move on to the next phase—eliminating distractions. In the next chapter, we'll dive into the art of **strategic ignorance**: learning what to say no to, how to say it, and why letting go of non-essential tasks can supercharge your success. Let's unlock the power of purposeful elimination and carve out space for what truly counts.

Chapter Eight

Eliminate: Mastering the Art of Strategic Ignorance

Eliminating distractions is the key to unlocking your true potential.

In a world full of endless notifications, urgent emails, and the ever-growing to-do list, learning to ignore the unimportant is not a luxury—it's a necessity. High achievers aren't people who do everything; they are people who focus on the right things and are brilliant at saying 'no' to the rest. This chapter will help you develop the skill of selective ignorance by implementing the Breakthrough Blocker Test and adopting the mindset needed to eliminate non-essential tasks. By the time you finish, you'll be equipped to say 'no' confidently, freeing up your time for what truly matters.

Implementing the Breakthrough Blocker Test

Not everything on your to-do list deserves your attention.

The Breakthrough Blocker Test is designed to help you differentiate between what moves the needle towards your goals and what's merely noise. Imagine standing in front of two doors: one leads to tangible progress, and the other to a spiral of busyness that leaves you exhausted but unfulfilled. The Breakthrough Blocker Test is your way of evaluating every task, project, or commitment by asking a few critical questions: Does this contribute directly to my breakthrough goals? Will this move me closer to the outcomes I want?

Start by taking your current list of commitments. For each one, consider whether it aligns with your larger objectives. If it doesn't, it goes on the 'ignore' list—no exceptions. This may feel uncomfortable at first, especially if you're used to doing everything asked of you. But remember, your breakthrough lies in your ability to focus, not in your ability to juggle.

Once you practice applying the Breakthrough Blocker Test consistently, you'll begin to notice how much of your day was previously dominated by tasks that don't matter. The goal here is not just to reduce your workload but to eliminate anything that takes time away from what's most crucial. You'll start to develop a new way of thinking—instead of defaulting to 'yes,' you'll ask yourself if saying 'yes' to a particular task means saying 'no' to your breakthroughs.

Strategies for Saying 'No' and Eliminating Non-Essential Tasks

'No' is not a negative word; it's your ticket to freedom.

For many, saying 'no' feels uncomfortable. It can come with a sense of guilt or anxiety about disappointing others. However, every 'yes' is also a 'no' to something else—often, it's a 'no' to your own priorities. To master the art of strategic ignorance, you have to become comfortable with the idea that saying 'no' is a powerful act of self-respect.

One effective strategy is to use the 'Positive No.' This involves affirming your commitment to your priorities while declining politely but firmly. For example, if a colleague asks you to join a project that doesn't align with your breakthrough goals, you could say, "I appreciate you thinking of me for this, but I'm focusing on other projects that align with my current objectives." This way, you aren't just turning someone down—you're communicating your focus and intent.

Another approach is setting clear boundaries. This means blocking out time for deep work and not letting interruptions in. Think of your time as precious real estate—if something isn't of high value, it doesn't get a spot. Learning phrases like, "I'm unable to commit to that right now," or "I have other priorities that require my attention," will also make saying 'no' feel less confrontational. It's not about being dismissive—it's about honoring your commitments to yourself.

These strategies will help you eliminate the non-essential and focus on what truly matters. As you get comfortable with these approaches, you'll notice a reduction in stress and an increase in your ability to make meaningful progress on your breakthrough goals.

Overcoming Guilt and Anxiety Associated with Task Elimination

Choosing what not to do is just as important as choosing what to do.

Saying 'no' often triggers guilt and anxiety, especially if you're used to being a people-pleaser or a go-getter who prides themselves on handling everything. But understand this—the guilt you feel is a byproduct of a culture that glorifies busyness. You've been conditioned to believe that being occupied is the same as being productive. To truly embrace selective ignorance, you need to challenge this belief.

One way to reframe this mindset is to think of yourself as the guardian of your time. If you allow yourself to feel guilty every time you refuse a task, you're handing over control of your life to others. By deciding what's truly important, you're not only protecting your time—you're protecting the energy that fuels your breakthroughs. Remind yourself that your time is finite, and every task you say 'yes' to must deserve a place in your schedule.

Another powerful mindset shift is to see 'no' as an investment in your future. Each time you decline a non-essential task, you're investing time into what matters most. It's helpful to reflect on past situations where saying 'yes' led to exhaustion or burnout. Use these experiences as a reminder that spreading yourself too thin prevents you from achieving your true potential.

It can also help to surround yourself with examples of people who have mastered this art. Most successful individuals, from CEOs to creatives, are deliberate about protecting their focus. Learn from their experiences and remind yourself that saying 'no' is an act of strength, not weakness.

The Power of Eliminating Non-Essentials

By eliminating the unnecessary, you create space for your greatness to emerge.

When you begin eliminating tasks that don't align with your breakthrough goals, you'll notice a shift—both in your productivity and your overall sense of well-being. This process isn't just about clearing your schedule; it's about changing the way you approach your entire career. You're no longer a reactive participant in your life, responding to every demand thrown your way. Instead, you become proactive, taking control of your focus and investing it where it counts.

This is where the magic happens. As you clear away the non-essentials, you'll find more mental clarity, creativity, and energy. This new space allows you to delve deeper into tasks that matter, rather than rushing through everything on your list. The satisfaction you get from completing high-value work far outweighs the fleeting satisfaction of checking off dozens of low-impact tasks.

When you eliminate the unnecessary, you also improve your ability to make better decisions. Without the constant mental clutter of unnecessary tasks, you have more bandwidth to think strategically, solve complex problems, and innovate. The very act of cutting down on busyness makes room for the work that requires focus and ingenuity—the kind of work that leads to breakthroughs.

The Breakthrough Blocker Test in Practice

Turning theory into practice is the path to real progress.

The Breakthrough Blocker Test is an invaluable tool, but like any tool, its power is in its application. Let's walk through a practical scenario where you apply the Breakthrough Blocker Test. Imagine you've been given the opportunity to join a new committee at work. It sounds interesting, but you're currently focused on a critical project that could significantly advance your career. Here's how you'd use the Breakthrough Blocker Test to decide.

First, ask yourself: **Does this committee align with my current breakthrough goals?** If the answer is no, then it's a clear sign that your answer should be 'no.' Next, consider the time commitment: **Will this new responsibility take away from my high-priority project?** If yes, then again, it needs to be ignored. Lastly, evaluate the opportunity cost: **If I take on this task, what will I be saying 'no' to?** If the answer is your most important work, then it's time to decline politely.

Practice makes perfect, and the more often you apply this test, the quicker and more intuitive it will become. Eventually, you won't even need to run through all the questions formally—you'll just know which tasks are worth your time and which aren't. The Breakthrough Blocker Test becomes an automatic filter, allowing you to maintain laser-like focus on your breakthrough goals.

Practical Tools for Eliminating Distractions

Strategic tools can help turn new habits into lasting change.

In addition to the Breakthrough Blocker Test, there are practical tools that can assist you in eliminating distractions and managing your workload effectively. One such tool is time-blocking. By scheduling dedicated time for deep, focused work, you create a non-negotiable commitment to yourself. Block out periods of your day when you won't take calls, check emails, or engage in meetings. During these blocks, focus solely on high-priority tasks.

Another helpful technique is creating an 'ignore list.' This list is just as important as your to-do list. Write down all the tasks, habits, or commitments that have been stealing your time and attention without providing real value. By making an 'ignore list,' you give yourself permission to let go of these distractions guilt-free. Keep it visible as a reminder of what you are intentionally choosing to disregard.

Consider using digital tools to reduce the clutter in your workday. Apps like Trello, Asana, or even just a well-organized Google Calendar can help you visually prioritize what's important. Email management tools that filter non-urgent messages into separate folders can also be a game-changer. The idea is to streamline your environment so that your focus is automatically drawn to what matters most.

Overcoming Resistance from Others

People may resist your newfound focus—stick to your commitment.

As you start saying 'no' to non-essential tasks, you may face resistance from others. Whether it's a boss who's used to you taking on everything, or colleagues who are accustomed to your constant support, it's normal to experience pushback. People like the status quo, especially when it benefits them. Your challenge will be to stay firm in your commitment to eliminate distractions.

It helps to communicate your reasons clearly. Explain that you are focusing on breakthrough goals that require deep work, and that by saying 'no' to certain requests, you're able to bring more value to the projects that truly matter. When people understand that your focus will ultimately lead to better results, they are often more supportive than you might expect.

Be prepared for moments where you'll need to reaffirm your boundaries. You might have someone insist that you take on something "just this once." These are the moments that test your resolve. Stick to your priorities. Politely but firmly explain your position, and remember—every time you give in, you dilute the power of your focus. Stay committed to your breakthrough goals, and others will eventually respect your boundaries.

Making Elimination a Habit

Eliminating distractions isn't a one-time action—it's a way of life.

Making elimination a habit requires consistency. It's easy to let small distractions creep back in if you're not vigilant. One effective method is to do a weekly review. Take time at the end of each week to evaluate how well you adhered to your focus goals. Did you take on any tasks that weren't aligned with your breakthroughs? What could you do differently next week to maintain clarity and focus?

Another habit to develop is practicing reflection. At the end of each day, consider whether you worked on your highest-priority tasks. If not, why? Did something unimportant steal your time? Use these reflections to adjust and improve continually. Over time, this daily reflection will help you internalize the process of elimination, making it a natural part of how you work.

Finally, celebrate the progress you make. Eliminating distractions is not easy, especially when you've been conditioned to say 'yes' to everything. Recognize the moments when you successfully protected your time for deep, meaningful work. Reward yourself for making choices that honor your breakthrough goals.

Time to Act...

Eliminating distractions is just one part of achieving your breakthrough—taking decisive action is the next.

In the next chapter, we'll explore how to transition from decision to action, maintaining momentum on your breakthrough journey. You'll learn strategies to overcome procrastination, keep your focus sharp, and consistently make progress towards your most important goals.

"The secret of success is to do the common thing uncommonly well."
- John D. Rockefeller Jr.

Chapter Nine

Act: From Decision to Breakthrough

The path from intention to action is where real change begins.

Intentions without action are like seeds left on the shelf—they hold potential but never grow. In this chapter, we'll explore how to bridge the gap between what you want to achieve and the actions that will bring it to life. This journey is about going from mere decision-making to executing consistently on the priorities that will truly make a difference in your career and life. You already know what you need to focus on—now it's time to make those priorities an unstoppable force.

Turning decisions into actions is what separates high achievers from dreamers. In the pages that follow, we'll equip you with tools and insights to build momentum, overcome the distractions that threaten your focus, and create consistent progress toward your most important goals. By learning how to maintain focus, beat procrastination, and celebrate each small step forward, you'll move from wishful thinking to tangible success. Ready to get started?

Techniques for Maintaining Focus on High-Priority Tasks

Staying focused in today's world can feel like swimming upstream. Information, notifications, and endless tasks bombard us from every direction. To maintain focus on what matters most, we need to understand that focus is both an art and a skill—one that requires deliberate practice and the right techniques.

One of the most effective ways to maintain focus on high-priority tasks is to create an environment that supports deep work. **Deep work** is the ability to focus without distraction on cognitively demanding tasks. When you arrange your workspace to minimize distractions, you prime yourself for greater productivity. This might mean clearing your physical workspace of clutter or turning off notifications on your devices. By doing this, you send a message to your brain that it's time to concentrate.

Another powerful strategy for maintaining focus is **time blocking**. Time blocking is the practice of scheduling dedicated time for your most important tasks and treating those time slots as non-negotiable. During these blocks, you focus solely on the task at hand—no emails, no social media, no interruptions. The key is to protect these time blocks fiercely, just as you would an important meeting. Time blocking not only helps you stay on track but also ensures that you make consistent progress on what really matters.

The Pomodoro Technique can also be incredibly helpful. This technique consists of dividing work into 25-minute segments, known as "Pomodoros," followed by brief breaks. This method involves breaking work into 25-minute intervals (called "Pomodoros") with short breaks in between. This structure helps maintain focus while giving your brain the rest it needs to stay sharp. By working in short bursts, you can keep your energy levels up and avoid the fatigue that often comes from trying to power through long, uninterrupted sessions. Additionally, the frequent breaks help refresh your mind, making it easier to re-engage with the task at hand with renewed focus. This technique can be especially useful for managing tasks that require sustained concentration, as it breaks them into manageable parts, making the workload feel less overwhelming. Over time, using the Pomodoro Technique can also help you better estimate how long certain tasks take, improving your planning skills and allowing for a more realistic approach to time management. The combination of focus, frequent rest, and the psychological benefit of working in shorter intervals makes the Pomodoro Technique a versatile tool for boosting productivity and sustaining motivation.

Maintaining focus also involves knowing when to say **no**. Every time you say yes to a low-value task, you're effectively saying no to something more important. Practicing selective ignorance—the conscious decision to ignore non-essential information—is one of the most powerful tools at your disposal. It allows you to keep your attention on what truly moves the needle and avoid getting sidetracked by things that don't matter.

Ultimately, maintaining focus on high-priority tasks comes down to your willingness to design your environment, schedule, and mindset around what matters most. The strategies above are practical ways to build a laser-like focus that will help you turn your intentions into meaningful actions.

Overcoming Procrastination and Resistance

Procrastination is one of the biggest barriers to taking action on high-priority tasks. It's not about laziness—it's often about fear, uncertainty, or simply feeling overwhelmed. Understanding why we procrastinate is the first step in overcoming it.

One common reason for procrastination is **fear of failure**. When a task feels important, the stakes feel high. The fear of not doing it well can paralyze us. To combat this, it helps to reframe failure as part of the learning process. Rather than seeing mistakes as setbacks, view them as opportunities for growth. The key is to take imperfect action—to start even if you don't feel ready, and adjust as you go. Progress is more important than perfection.

Another cause of procrastination is the feeling of being overwhelmed by the size of the task. When a goal feels too big, it's easy to put off starting. The solution here is to **break the task into smaller, manageable pieces**. By focusing on one small step at a time, you can reduce the intimidation factor and start building momentum. Each small step forward will create a sense of accomplishment, which in turn makes it easier to keep going.

Accountability can also be a powerful motivator. Sharing your goals with a trusted friend, mentor, or colleague creates a sense of responsibility to follow through. Knowing that someone else is aware of your intentions can give you the extra push needed to overcome resistance. You can even take this a step further by setting up regular check-ins or progress updates.

Another helpful strategy is to use **temptation bundling**, which involves pairing a task you might procrastinate on with an activity you enjoy. For example, if you struggle to sit down and work on a report, you could pair that work with listening to your favorite music or enjoying a good cup of coffee. This technique makes the task more appealing and reduces the initial resistance to getting started.

Lastly, **visualizing the end result** can help overcome procrastination. Take a moment to picture what it will feel like when you complete the task. Imagine the sense of relief, the pride in your work, and the benefits that will come from finishing. By focusing on the positive outcomes, you can motivate yourself to push past the initial hesitation and get started.

Tracking Progress and Celebrating Small Wins

Tracking progress is essential for maintaining motivation and keeping your momentum alive. It's easy to lose sight of how far you've come, especially when you're in the thick of things. That's why keeping track of your achievements—even the small ones—can make a huge difference.

One effective way to track progress is by using a **visual tracker**, such as a progress chart or a checklist. Physically seeing your progress can be incredibly satisfying and motivating. Whether it's crossing items off a list or filling in a chart, the visual representation of your accomplishments can give you a tangible sense of achievement.

Journaling is another valuable tool for tracking progress. At the end of each day or week, take a few minutes to write down what you accomplished, what challenges you faced, and what you plan to focus on next. This practice not only helps you reflect on your progress but also allows you to identify patterns—both positive and negative—in your work habits. By understanding these patterns, you can make adjustments to improve your productivity and focus over time.

It's also crucial to **celebrate small wins**. Too often, we focus only on the big goals and overlook the smaller milestones along the way. Celebrating small wins helps to reinforce positive behavior and keeps you motivated. This doesn't mean you need to throw a party for every little task you complete—it can be as simple as giving yourself a short break, treating yourself to something you enjoy, or sharing your progress with someone who supports you. Another way to celebrate small wins is to create a rewards system for yourself. For example, after completing a significant number of small tasks, you could reward yourself with something more substantial, like a special meal or a day off. Recognizing these wins can also involve taking a moment to reflect on how much closer you are to your bigger goals. By pausing and acknowledging these steps forward, you are mentally reinforcing your progress, which can have a powerful impact on your overall mindset and motivation. Whether it's a verbal acknowledgment, a written note in your journal, or a simple smile of satisfaction, celebrating these moments helps maintain enthusiasm and creates a sense of ongoing achievement.

The idea behind celebrating small wins is to create a positive feedback loop. Each time you acknowledge a small success, you get a boost of motivation that helps you tackle the next task. This steady accumulation of small victories is what ultimately leads to major breakthroughs. By regularly recognizing these wins, you condition yourself to stay committed even when the larger goal feels far off. Remember, success is not about one giant leap—it's about the consistent, steady steps you take every day. These small steps build resilience and confidence, making the bigger challenges more manageable and less intimidating. The more you celebrate progress, the more you develop a growth-oriented mindset that sees value in every effort, no matter how small.

Tracking your progress and celebrating your wins are not just about feeling good—they're also about maintaining momentum and reinforcing the behaviors that will lead to your breakthrough. By recognizing how far you've come, you build the confidence needed to keep going, even when the journey gets tough. Additionally, celebrating these wins creates a positive association with the effort you put in, making it easier to dive into the next task. Momentum is built step by step, and the act of celebrating keeps the energy alive, especially during challenging times. It serves as a reminder that progress is happening, and it keeps your motivation levels high. Recognizing small victories also helps you stay focused on the process rather than getting lost in the enormity of your ultimate goals, which can often feel overwhelming.

Conclusion: Making Consistent Progress on High-Priority Actions

In this chapter, we've explored the journey from decision to action. We've covered how to maintain focus on what truly matters, how to overcome the natural resistance that often keeps us from taking action, and the importance of tracking progress and celebrating our wins along the way. The key takeaway here is that consistent progress comes from creating an environment that supports your goals, building habits that keep you on track, and recognizing every step forward—no matter how small.

Action is where dreams take shape. It's where your plans and intentions come to life and become something tangible. The most successful people are not those who never struggle, but those who learn to keep moving forward despite the challenges. By applying the strategies in this chapter, you're building a foundation for ongoing progress and setting yourself up for career-defining breakthroughs.

Refine and Improve...

In the next chapter, we'll explore how to refine your approach over time—ensuring that your strategies continue to evolve and improve as you do. We'll look at how to measure the effectiveness of your actions and make adjustments that lead to even greater success. Let's keep building momentum and moving closer to the breakthroughs that await you.

Chapter Ten

Refine: Evolving Your Breakthrough Strategy

Establishing a system for continuous improvement is the key to sustaining career breakthroughs.

Achieving a breakthrough is an incredible moment, but staying at the top requires a process for ongoing growth. Just like the greatest athletes don't stop training after a major win, professionals must keep refining their approach to maintain and build upon their success. This chapter will guide you through creating a system that allows you to stay agile and aligned with your goals, no matter how the career landscape shifts.

Let's dive into how you can maintain a mindset of continuous improvement and why this is crucial for sustainable success.

Establishing a System for Continuous Improvement

Refinement isn't about perfection; it's about growth. A key part of evolving your strategy is building a feedback loop—a process that allows you to continuously assess where you are, what's working, and what needs adjusting. This is how you stay sharp, relevant, and always ready to take the next step toward greater success.

The idea of a feedback loop isn't new, but it's often overlooked in personal career development. Many professionals set a goal, achieve it, and then drift into autopilot, assuming the success will continue on its own. However, success isn't a one-time action; it's a practice. Establishing a system for continuous improvement means building in deliberate moments of reflection and action. Think of it as a regular audit of your strategy: What's serving you well? What's no longer effective? Where are the new opportunities for growth?

One practical way to establish this system is to schedule a regular monthly review—a time dedicated solely to analyzing your priorities, outcomes, and actions. Are the tasks you're working on still aligned with your overall goals? Are there better, more efficient ways to approach them? Use these sessions to recalibrate and refocus. Continuous improvement is not about making massive changes every month, but instead, making small, consistent tweaks that accumulate into substantial, career-defining differences over time.

The beauty of this process is that it keeps you proactive rather than reactive. Instead of waiting until something goes wrong to make a change, you're always iterating, always refining. You're evolving alongside your goals and the shifting demands of your career.

Adapting the Method to Changing Career Landscapes

The world of work is constantly evolving, and what worked well in the past may not serve you in the future. Adaptability is crucial—the ability to tweak, shift, and pivot your strategies as new challenges and opportunities arise will determine how far you can go. This is where the Breakthrough Blocker Method comes into play as more than just a one-time fix; it's a tool for continuous adaptation.

To adapt your strategy effectively, you must stay informed about trends in your industry and remain open to the idea that change is not just inevitable but an opportunity. Adapting isn't simply about responding to crises; it's about proactively positioning yourself to take advantage of new possibilities. For example, consider how technological advances or shifting market demands might create opportunities for you to reassess your current priorities.

A helpful approach here is scenario planning. Scenario planning is where you anticipate different possible futures and outline how you might respond to each. This proactive approach means that, rather than being blindsided by change, you're prepared to pivot and use change to your advantage.

Think of your career as a ship—you are the captain steering towards a destination. The sea can be unpredictable: the tides, the wind, and even unexpected storms. To navigate effectively, you need to adjust your sails and your course. Similarly, adapting your career strategies means continuously fine-tuning them to keep moving in the right direction, regardless of what the environment throws at you.

Metrics for Measuring the Effectiveness of Your New Approach

The concept of continuous improvement requires not only a willingness to change but also a way to measure whether your changes are having the desired impact. Establishing clear metrics for evaluating your progress is critical to ensuring you are genuinely improving rather than just making changes for change's sake.

One powerful metric is to evaluate the alignment of your daily tasks with your long-term goals. Are the actions you're taking each day contributing to the big picture? If not, then your time may be misaligned, and it's time to recalibrate. Tracking your progress against your long-term goals provides a concrete way to see how effective your current strategy is. Are you closer to your objectives than you were last month? Are you seeing meaningful progress, or have you plateaued?

Another effective metric is to assess the quality of your work versus the quantity of tasks completed. Many people equate being busy with being productive, but the real question is whether your actions are contributing to the breakthroughs you want. Quality is far more important than sheer volume when it comes to the actions that lead to significant career growth. Ask yourself: Have my most important tasks been completed with the focus and attention they deserve? Is what I'm producing creating value?

Additionally, gather feedback from trusted peers or mentors. Sometimes it's difficult to see the full picture from within your own experience. External feedback provides a new lens through which you can view your progress, offering insights you might have missed. Create a circle of trusted colleagues or mentors who can offer honest feedback on your progress and help you keep your breakthroughs aligned with the shifting demands of your career.

The Power of Small Tweaks Over Time

Continuous improvement isn't about drastic overhauls; it's about making small, deliberate changes that lead to big outcomes over time. When we think of change, we often imagine it as a monumental shift, but in reality, the most sustainable improvements come from small adjustments made consistently. This mindset shift—from expecting sudden, massive transformations to appreciating the power of gradual refinement—is what will set you apart.

Think about an elite athlete fine-tuning their performance. It's rarely about changing their entire routine overnight. Instead, they'll make tiny adjustments: tweaking their diet, refining their form, or adjusting their training intensity. These changes compound over time, and before you know it, they're breaking personal records. Your career growth is no different.

The key here is persistence. It can be tempting to chase a quick fix or a sudden career boost, but the truth is that sustained success comes from consistently showing up and refining your approach. The small tweaks you make today—whether that's eliminating a time-wasting activity, improving a key skill, or simply better aligning your priorities—will accumulate and lead to significant breakthroughs down the line.

This concept is particularly important when you feel stuck or stagnant. Often, the solution isn't a massive change but rather a small shift that reenergizes your approach. Perhaps it's dedicating just 10 extra minutes a day to learning a new skill or deciding to let go of a task that's no longer serving you. Small actions, repeated consistently, are what lead to meaningful evolution.

Common Misconceptions About Refinement and Growth

There's a common misconception that refining your strategy means you got it wrong the first time. This couldn't be further from the truth. Refinement is not an admission of failure; it's an acknowledgment of the dynamic nature of success. The world changes, industries shift, and what worked well yesterday may need tweaking today. It's about embracing evolution rather than standing still.

Another misconception is that continuous improvement requires constant change. Improvement doesn't mean you have to overhaul everything all the time. In fact, sometimes the best way to improve is to double down on what's already working well. The goal of continuous refinement is to build on your strengths while identifying and mitigating your weaknesses.

People also often think that they need a perfect plan to start refining their career approach, but that's just another way to stall progress. You don't need to wait for the perfect circumstances. The best way to refine your strategy is to start now, with whatever tools and insights you have, and allow the process to evolve as you learn more about what works for you.

Staying Motivated During the Refinement Process

The journey of continuous refinement can be challenging, especially when progress feels slow or invisible. There will be times when it feels like you're putting in the effort but not seeing immediate results, and that can be disheartening. However, maintaining motivation during this process is key to long-term success.

One effective way to stay motivated is to celebrate small wins. Refinement isn't about achieving big wins every day; it's about those small, meaningful steps that accumulate over time. Recognize the value in those tiny successes—whether it's finally saying no to a non-essential task or completing a challenging project that aligns with your goals. Celebrating these moments keeps you focused on the progress you're making.

Another way to keep motivation high is to maintain a growth mindset. Understand that every misstep or challenge is an opportunity to learn and refine further. Adopting a mindset where every experience, both good and bad, becomes a stepping stone rather than an obstacle will help you navigate the ups and downs of the refinement process with resilience and positivity.

Finally, surround yourself with others who are also committed to growth. This could be a community of peers, mentors, or even just a few trusted friends. When you're feeling stuck or unsure, leaning on others who understand your journey can provide new insights, encouragement, and the motivation to keep going.

Growth doesn't have to be a solitary process—it's much more fulfilling when shared with others.

Making Refinement a Lifelong Habit

Refinement isn't just a phase; it's a lifelong habit that leads to sustained success. Once you've achieved your initial career breakthrough, you might be tempted to rest on your laurels. After all, you worked hard to get there. But true success comes from recognizing that each milestone is just one point on an ongoing journey. There will always be new skills to learn, new challenges to face, and new heights to reach.

To make refinement a habit, schedule it into your life just like any other priority. Whether it's a monthly reflection session, a quarterly review, or a yearly strategy retreat, make time to assess where you are and where you're heading. Use this time to ask yourself the tough questions: Am I still aligned with my long-term goals? Are there any new opportunities I should explore? What changes can I make today to ensure I keep progressing?

The commitment to lifelong refinement also means being open to feedback and learning continuously. Whether it's through formal education, informal mentorship, or simply learning from the people around you, every opportunity to grow is an opportunity to refine your strategy. Keep learning, stay curious, and never be satisfied with the status quo.

Your Momentum Flywheel...

Refinement is a journey that keeps you aligned, adaptable, and continuously moving toward greater success. As you grow and evolve, the ability to refine your strategy ensures that each breakthrough builds upon the last, creating a momentum that propels you forward. Now that we've explored how to refine and adapt your strategy, let's look at how you can leverage your initial breakthroughs to fuel exponential growth in the next chapter.

"The race is not always to the swift, but to those who keep running."
- Unknown

Chapter Eleven

Accelerating Your Success Flywheel

Success isn't just about making it to the top—it's about building momentum that keeps you growing long after you've reached your initial goals.

In the pursuit of career success, the real magic begins when you turn those initial achievements into a cycle of continued growth. This chapter explores how leveraging early wins can create a self-sustaining momentum, like a flywheel that, once in motion, becomes almost unstoppable. By understanding how to strategically amplify those first small victories, you'll learn to harness exponential growth, ensuring that each success fuels the next and propels you even further. This chapter provides practical tools and advanced techniques to make clarity and focus not just something you achieve once, but a long-term habit. You'll see how decluttering your professional life allows new opportunities to shine through, helping you achieve growth beyond what you imagined.

The journey to sustained career success begins with understanding how to make your wins work for you, growing them into bigger, bolder breakthroughs.

Leveraging Initial Wins for Exponential Growth

The biggest mistake many professionals make is thinking that their early successes are the end of the story. In truth, those wins are just the opening chapter in a much larger narrative. Each achievement is a foundation upon which bigger successes can be built—if you know how to harness it properly.

Think about your career milestones as stepping stones across a river. Each stone you place carefully sets up the next, allowing you to cross further. One early win, no matter how small, can be the perfect base for future opportunities if you leverage it effectively. But what does it mean to leverage an initial win? It starts with recognizing its value. Many people hit a milestone and simply move on, treating it like a box to tick off rather than an asset to utilize. The key to real growth lies in recognizing that every success, no matter how modest, is a potential launchpad.

Once you've acknowledged the significance of your win, take a step back and ask yourself: "How can I amplify this?" Whether it's a new skill, a promotion, or a successful project, there's almost always a way to use it as leverage. For example, if you've successfully launched a project that got positive feedback, share that success—internally and externally. Talk about it in meetings, on social media, and even in casual conversations. Not only does this give you recognition, but it helps position you as someone who takes initiative and delivers results. The more people see you in this light, the more opportunities you will attract to build upon this foundation.

The power of leveraging initial wins lies in compounding. Each time you grow from a win, that growth is exponential, creating a multiplier effect for all future achievements. Imagine a snowball rolling downhill, gaining size and speed. Your small wins, if treated with care and strategy, work in much the same way. As these small wins gain momentum, they compound into something bigger, leading to greater opportunities and increasing returns.

Another crucial aspect of leveraging wins is learning from them. Every success holds lessons that can teach you more about your strengths, capabilities, and potential pathways. By analyzing what made a win successful, you uncover repeatable strategies—those actions or habits that have a direct impact on your progress. Knowing what works makes it easier to replicate and grow those successes.

Advanced Techniques for Maintaining Clarity and Focus

The initial buzz of a new achievement can be thrilling, but the challenge is to maintain that level of focus and energy long after the excitement has worn off. One of the greatest threats to sustained growth is losing clarity—when your attention begins to scatter, you become less effective, and your momentum falters. Advanced focus techniques are essential to keep your flywheel spinning.

1. The Power of Intentional Reflection

To sustain your progress, you need to be intentional about what you focus on and when. One powerful technique is **intentional reflection**. Instead of simply moving from one project to the next, set aside time to reflect on what you've done well and what could be improved. Reflection isn't just about learning from mistakes; it's also about understanding your strengths. Ask yourself: "What went right? Why did it go right? How can I build on this?" These questions can help you stay on track and identify which actions will lead to greater success.

This reflection can be done weekly or monthly. Create a simple ritual for it—find a quiet space, bring a notebook, and write out your thoughts. By doing so, you become more deliberate in maintaining the clarity that drives your progress.

2. Building a Clarity Checklist

A practical way to maintain focus is to develop a **clarity checklist**. This list will include key priorities and non-negotiables that align with your career goals. As you grow, opportunities will multiply, and it will be easy to overcommit or be distracted. A clarity checklist keeps you grounded, ensuring you remain aligned with your core objectives rather than chasing every shiny new opportunity.

3. Embrace the "Not Now" Mindset

Another advanced technique for clarity is cultivating a "not now" mindset. Often, it's not about saying "no" forever to opportunities but about knowing which ones to defer. If an opportunity doesn't align with your current focus, categorize it as "not now."

This practice reduces overwhelm while keeping the door open for the future—when it makes more strategic sense for your goals.

4. Mental Decluttering Practices

Over time, mental clutter—unfinished projects, unfulfilled ideas, or unmade decisions—can sap your energy and clarity. To maintain sharp focus, schedule regular mental decluttering sessions where you review your ongoing projects and commitments. Eliminate, delegate, or defer those that don't contribute directly to your immediate priorities.

The goal of these advanced techniques is to help you stay aligned with your primary purpose, ensuring that you channel your time and energy into what truly matters.

Identifying New Opportunities in a Decluttered Professional Life

With a decluttered mind and a focused approach, something wonderful happens—opportunities that were previously hidden start to come into view. Just as decluttering a room makes space for new things, decluttering your professional life creates room for new, exciting opportunities.

When you eliminate distractions, you'll be amazed at what surfaces. It's like clearing away the weeds in a garden and discovering the beautiful flowers underneath. The key to identifying these new opportunities is being present and paying attention to the gaps—both in your work and in the broader field. Decluttering gives you the bandwidth to think beyond just surviving your workday; it allows you to innovate, explore, and grow.

1. Practice Opportunity Scanning

With a clear head, dedicate time each week to a simple exercise called **opportunity scanning**. This involves spending just 10 to 15 minutes reviewing trends in your industry, networking, and reflecting on new skills that could be beneficial. Opportunity scanning is about having the mental and emotional space to notice what's happening around you that might align with your goals or spark your interest.

2. Connect with Innovators

Being connected to innovative people in your industry is another fantastic way to identify new opportunities. Once you've decluttered your professional commitments, you have more space to reach out, connect, and brainstorm with others who are also looking to make an impact. These connections can open doors you may never have even considered.

3. Develop a Vision Board for Opportunities

A fun yet effective tool is to create a **vision board** that captures future opportunities you're excited about—whether it's a new skill, a collaboration, or even an entirely new career path. This keeps those opportunities front and center, ensuring that your focus stays on growth areas even as you pursue your day-to-day priorities.

4. Play the Long Game

Finally, identifying new opportunities often requires the willingness to play the long game. Be patient and understand that sometimes the seeds you plant today won't bear fruit until months or even years later. By maintaining a decluttered, intentional focus, you create fertile ground for these opportunities to eventually take root.

Creating a Flywheel of Success

The idea of a flywheel is simple: it takes some initial effort to get it spinning, but once it gains momentum, it keeps going with minimal input. Your career growth can work the same way. By investing time and energy in leveraging wins, staying focused, and creating space for new opportunities, you build a career flywheel that sustains itself.

Think of your initial achievements as the push that gets the flywheel going. Each time you leverage a success—by sharing it, using it as a stepping stone, or learning from it—you give that flywheel another spin. The more consistent you are in doing this, the faster it spins, creating energy and momentum that will take you further with less effort.

1. Make Your Wins Public

One way to keep your flywheel spinning is to make your successes visible. Share them, both with your team and with your broader professional community. This isn't about bragging—it's about reinforcing your role as someone who gets results, attracts opportunities, and is moving forward. Recognition attracts momentum, and the more people know about your achievements, the more you'll be positioned for new opportunities.

2. Keep Learning and Adapting

A key part of creating a flywheel is maintaining an **adaptation mindset**. The world changes quickly, and what worked yesterday might not work tomorrow. Regularly updating your skills, staying in tune with industry shifts, and adapting your strategy keeps your flywheel in motion. In a sense, your career flywheel isn't static—it's evolving. Each success builds upon an adaptable foundation that helps you stay relevant and agile.

3. Celebrate and Replicate Your Wins

Don't underestimate the importance of **celebrating small wins**. Celebrating reminds you why you're doing what you're doing and helps you build positive energy, which keeps you motivated. Once you celebrate, think about replication: "What did I do to achieve this, and how can I do it again—better?" Replication turns small wins into habits, and habits are the true engine behind the flywheel of success.

Maintaining Your Momentum

Once your career flywheel is in motion, maintaining that momentum becomes your primary focus. The good news? Each success generates energy that makes the next push easier. But it still requires intentional action.

1. Consistent Goal Setting

Set goals that are always just a little bit beyond your current reach. These goals keep you moving, pushing yourself to learn and grow. Make sure that each goal builds on your previous successes, using them as stepping stones to the next level.

2. Develop Systems, Not Just Goals

Goals give you something to aim for, but **systems** are what keep your flywheel turning day in and day out. A system is a repeatable set of actions—whether it's a morning routine that sets you up for a productive day, a weekly planning session, or a habit of checking in on your progress. Systems sustain you during those periods when motivation wanes.

3. Find Your Community

Success doesn't happen in a vacuum. Finding a **community** that supports your growth helps keep your momentum alive. This can be a group of like-minded peers, a mentor who pushes you forward, or a network of professionals who inspire you. The people you surround yourself with can provide insights, accountability, and encouragement—all essential for maintaining your flywheel.

4. Adapt and Overcome Setbacks

Even the most well-oiled flywheels encounter resistance from time to time. Whether it's a setback in your career, a project that fails, or personal circumstances that slow your progress, the key is to **adapt and overcome**. Use setbacks as learning opportunities—ask yourself, "What can I take away from this experience?" Successful people aren't those who avoid setbacks; they're those who use them as fuel for growth.

Conclusion: Keep Spinning Towards Growth

Building a career flywheel is about creating self-sustaining momentum that powers you through your journey, growing stronger with each spin. Leveraging initial wins, maintaining clarity, decluttering to find new opportunities, and using advanced focus techniques are all essential components of this process. When you recognize the value in every success—no matter how small—and find ways to amplify and build upon it, you create a force that drives you forward.

As you continue on this journey, remember that momentum compounds. The more you leverage, celebrate, and replicate your successes, the more unstoppable your career growth becomes. With the right tools and the right mindset, your flywheel can keep spinning towards new, exciting heights of success.

Navigating Your Career...

In the next chapter we'll explore how to manage the complexities that often arise in a fast-paced career. You'll learn to navigate high-stakes decisions, major projects, and the unexpected turns that come your way—all while maintaining the momentum you've worked so hard to build.

Chapter Twelve

Navigating Career Complexities

The modern workplace demands not only skill but also the ability to adapt swiftly and intelligently.

In a career landscape where responsibilities are ever-evolving and stakes are high, the ability to navigate complexities with grace and purpose has become the definitive skill for sustained success. For those who juggle multiple projects, roles, and unexpected shifts, there is an urgent need to identify what truly matters and how to stay effective without burning out. In this chapter, we'll explore the strategies necessary for applying the Breakthrough Blocker Method to complex career challenges, showing you how to manage multiple responsibilities, make effective decisions under pressure, and embrace change as a catalyst for growth. Let's dive into how to do more of what matters and less of what doesn't in the most demanding moments of your professional journey.

Ultimately, thriving in career complexity comes down to knowing where to focus, even when everything feels urgent.

Applying the Breakthrough Blocker Method to High-Stakes Decisions

High-stakes decisions are part and parcel of career growth, but they often come with fear, doubt, and the heavy weight of potential consequences. The Breakthrough Blocker Method is designed to provide clarity, especially in these high-pressure situations, by helping you focus only on what is truly essential.

The first step to mastering high-stakes decisions is to **clarify your objectives**. When faced with a tough decision, it's easy to get lost in details or become paralyzed by the fear of getting it wrong. To counteract this, make it a habit to start with the end in mind: what outcome are you hoping to achieve? Write it down if needed. By being absolutely clear about your objectives, you narrow the field of options and remove unnecessary distractions. The Breakthrough Blocker Method emphasizes this clarity because it serves as the foundation for every subsequent choice.

Next, **evaluate your options based on impact and alignment with your goals**. Not all opportunities are equal, and not every decision point demands equal attention. A key part of the Breakthrough Blocker philosophy is that strategic ignorance can be powerful—ignoring the less significant to focus on the potential breakthroughs. Use this mindset to evaluate which of your available options moves you closer to your career goals in a meaningful way. Often, people end up overwhelmed by decisions because they give equal weight to trivial choices as they do to those that truly matter.

The last critical part of making high-stakes decisions involves **testing assumptions**. High-stakes often mean high uncertainty, and that means assumptions could derail your thought process. To manage this, take a moment to list out the assumptions you're making and think critically about their validity. Could these assumptions be wrong? What evidence do you have to support them? By consciously examining your assumptions, you reduce the risk of moving forward based on faulty logic, ensuring that your final decision is based on a solid understanding of the reality at hand.

When you use the Breakthrough Blocker Method in high-stakes situations, you're not just making decisions—you're making the right ones, anchored in a clear understanding of your objectives and priorities.

Strategies for Managing Multiple Major Projects or Roles

Balancing multiple projects or even multiple roles at work is not an easy feat. However, it's often an inevitable part of moving up in your career—the higher you climb, the more responsibilities you juggle. In these situations, mastering how to categorize your commitments and prioritize effectively is essential to maintain productivity without compromising your mental and physical well-being.

A key strategy in the Breakthrough Blocker Method for managing multiple responsibilities is **mapping your professional landscape**. This starts with a detailed task audit—literally making a list of everything on your plate, big and small. This isn't just about writing down tasks, but about categorizing them by urgency, importance, and alignment with your long-term goals. Are you dealing with day-to-day tasks, or are there projects that could lead to major breakthroughs? By laying everything out in front of you, you can visualize where your energy is being directed and how well it aligns with your top priorities. Again, if you have made these lists in previous chapters, you can reference them, reassess them, update them, revise them, and/or upgrade them to use here.

Once you've mapped your landscape, it's time to **apply the principles of selective ignorance**. You can't do everything well, especially when juggling multiple responsibilities. The Breakthrough Blocker Test asks you to examine which of these tasks are truly worth your attention and which can be delegated, delayed, or dropped altogether. This selective approach is crucial for focusing your limited energy on what yields the greatest value. There is power in saying "no"—it protects your time and mental bandwidth for what's genuinely meaningful.

To keep momentum, **time-blocking for specific roles or projects** is an invaluable tool. Create clear boundaries in your calendar dedicated to each major responsibility. This means carving out set times of day or week specifically allocated to focus on a particular project or role. By reducing mental switching between different tasks, you maintain deeper focus, which significantly enhances both the quality of work and your efficiency. When you are managing multiple roles, this discipline ensures that nothing critical falls through the cracks, and you maintain consistent progress.

Ultimately, managing multiple projects effectively comes down to knowing your limits and fiercely protecting the time and energy for what matters most.

Adapting to Rapid Change and Unexpected Career Shifts

The professional world is constantly evolving, and the ability to adapt to change is what separates those who thrive from those who merely survive. Unexpected changes can be daunting, whether they involve a shift in company direction, a sudden promotion, or market disruptions that make your current skills less relevant. However, the Breakthrough Blocker Method provides you with tools to not only adapt but also to grow in these moments of unpredictability.

The first thing to do when faced with rapid change is **to re-assess your priorities quickly and effectively**. Changes, by their nature, can render your existing priorities obsolete. The Breakthrough Blocker Method encourages you to return to the CLEAR framework, specifically revisiting the "Categorize" and "List Priorities" steps. What was once important may no longer be as relevant in the new context, so adjusting quickly ensures you're not wasting energy on goals that no longer serve your future. The faster you can realign your actions with the new direction, the sooner you'll regain a sense of control.

Embracing a growth mindset is also pivotal when dealing with change. A sudden shift can trigger resistance—especially if it pushes you out of your comfort zone. The truth is, growth happens on the edge of discomfort, and having the perspective that every challenge is an opportunity to learn changes how you react to unexpected shifts. When you see each change as a step toward personal and professional growth, you'll find the motivation to engage fully with it rather than resist it. The Breakthrough Blocker Method, with its focus on breaking free from non-essential distractions, allows you to spend more time embracing and learning from these changes.

Finally, **maintain open communication with key stakeholders** during times of transition. Whether the change is an industry shift or an internal reorganization, it's essential to keep the lines of communication open with your team, managers, or clients. This transparency helps everyone involved adjust expectations and offers a clear picture of how roles or responsibilities are evolving. When people are informed, they feel included, and it also provides you with a support system to navigate the change without feeling isolated.

Adapting successfully means making changes thoughtfully and remaining proactive in both mindset and communication, turning potentially challenging moments into significant opportunities for your career.

Practical Application: Action Steps for Navigating Complexity

Let's make the concepts in this chapter actionable by diving into specific steps you can take to navigate complexity in your career more effectively:

1. **Clarify Objectives for High-Stakes Decisions**:
   - Write down your top three career objectives.

- When faced with a high-stakes decision, evaluate which option best aligns with these objectives.

2. **Conduct a Task Audit**:
    - List all ongoing projects and roles.
    - Use categories like "urgent," "important," and "alignment with long-term goals" to classify these tasks.
3. **Apply Selective Ignorance**:
    - For each task or project, ask: Is this essential for my breakthrough?
    - Delegate, delay, or drop anything that doesn't make the cut.
4. **Time-Block for Projects and Roles**:
    - Dedicate specific blocks in your calendar for focused work on each role.
    - Stick to these blocks to avoid task-switching and maintain high-quality output.
5. **Reassess Priorities During Change**:
    - When changes arise, revisit your top priorities immediately.
    - Be willing to let go of what no longer aligns to make room for new, more important goals.

6. **Adopt a Growth Mindset**:
   - Write down one lesson learned from each challenging change you've faced in the past month.
   - Keep a "growth journal" to record how you're evolving with every new challenge.
7. **Communicate During Transition**:
   - Set up regular check-ins with your team during significant changes.
   - Be transparent about what's shifting, why it's happening, and how you plan to adapt.

These practical steps can help you transform what might feel like overwhelming career complexity into a structured approach that you can manage, adapt to, and thrive within.

Building Resilience for Career Complexity

Navigating career complexities successfully also requires building **resilience**. Resilience isn't just about withstanding challenges; it's about developing an attitude that allows you to grow stronger after each challenge you face. In a demanding career, setbacks are inevitable—whether they come in the form of missed opportunities, conflicts, or changes beyond your control. The Breakthrough Blocker Method is particularly suited to building resilience because it encourages you to focus only on what is meaningful, cutting away the mental clutter that makes setbacks feel insurmountable.

One of the best ways to cultivate resilience is through **small, consistent wins**. Progress fuels resilience. By setting achievable goals and consistently hitting them, you build a sense of forward movement. This can be as simple as setting a daily focus that aligns with your overall career objectives—perhaps it's finally delegating a task that has been draining your energy or making progress on a project that will elevate your professional standing. Each win, however small, adds up to a feeling of competence and control, which in turn enhances resilience.

Another key component of resilience is **maintaining perspective**. Often, we get overwhelmed because we see challenges as permanent or pervasive. Taking a step back and recognizing that a particular complexity or setback is temporary allows you to address it calmly and rationally. Perspective can also come from remembering that every challenge carries with it the opportunity to improve—each complexity is a chance to refine your prioritization methods, learn a new skill, or reassert your focus on what matters most.

Finally, **leverage your support system**. Resilience doesn't mean going it alone. Whether it's a mentor, peers, or a trusted friend, having people you can talk to when the going gets tough is invaluable. They can offer insights, provide encouragement, or simply lend a listening ear. When navigating complex professional scenarios, knowing you have people to lean on can make a world of difference.

Building resilience isn't about eliminating challenges but about becoming better equipped to face them and come out stronger on the other side.

Extend the Breakthrough Blocker Method...

Now that you've learned how to manage high-stakes decisions, juggle multiple roles, and embrace change, it's time to take these skills a step further. In the next chapter, we'll focus on how to extend the Breakthrough Blocker Method beyond your own career—guiding your team and your organization towards achieving breakthroughs that will benefit everyone involved. Let's explore how to become not just a high-achieving individual, but a breakthrough-driven leader who inspires others to prioritize and succeed.

"To win in horse racing, you don't always need to be the fastest. You just need to finish first."
– Unknown

Chapter Thirteen

The Breakthrough-Driven Leader

To truly make an impact, you must move beyond personal success and focus on collective breakthroughs.

In today's professional landscape, career success is often seen as an individual pursuit—the result of hard work, personal sacrifices, and a relentless focus on self-improvement. But what happens when you reach that pinnacle? You start to realize that genuine, lasting success is about more than just individual milestones. It's about lifting others with you, becoming a catalyst for change, and inspiring those around you to also reach their fullest potential. This chapter will help you transition from being solely an individual contributor to becoming a leader who fosters team breakthroughs.

It's time to extend your impact, going from just winning personally to ensuring that everyone around you is winning, too.

Transitioning from Individual Contributor to Breakthrough Catalyst

The leap from individual contributor to a leader capable of inspiring breakthroughs is often one of the most challenging transformations in a professional career. It involves a shift in focus—from doing great work yourself to enabling others to do the same. This isn't just about handing over tasks; it's about mindset, leadership, and creating an environment where breakthroughs aren't just possible—they're inevitable.

Imagine your career as a ladder. When you're climbing, it's all about your hands on the rungs, your feet making each step up. But when you become a leader, your role changes. Now, it's about holding the ladder steady, even reaching down to help others climb. For a breakthrough-driven leader, success is measured not by how far they climb alone, but by how many others they bring along to the top.

To transition effectively, start by reassessing your priorities. It's tempting to continue focusing solely on individual achievements—after all, those are what got you here. But a leader must measure success differently. Rather than individual accolades, your victories are now tied to the achievements of the people you lead. A key part of this shift is understanding what motivates those around you. Take time to know your team, their goals, and what they need to grow. When your focus shifts to enabling others to succeed, you pave the way for collective breakthroughs, ones that far exceed what you could achieve alone.

The most impactful leaders are those who have redefined their idea of success. When your focus becomes nurturing growth in others, you are no longer just a high-performer; you are the catalyst for an entire culture of excellence.

Inspiring and Guiding Teams to Adopt Prioritization Strategies

One of the biggest challenges as a leader is to get your team to understand the value of strategic prioritization. The Breakthrough Blocker Method, which you've mastered for your personal growth, can now become a tool for enabling your team to achieve collective success. But it's not just about telling them what to do—it's about inspiring them to see the value in the practice and making it a part of their own professional lives.

The truth is, most professionals struggle with prioritization. They're overwhelmed by the sheer volume of tasks, caught up in the false allure of busyness, and unsure how to distinguish what truly matters from what doesn't. As their leader, you have the power to change that. Start by communicating openly about your journey. Share how adopting a prioritization strategy shifted your trajectory, allowing you to focus only on the tasks that drive real progress. When your team hears about your experience—including the struggles, the revelations, and the triumphs—they're more likely to trust the process and engage with it.

But inspiration is only the beginning. Effective guidance is crucial. You need to provide your team with clear, actionable tools to identify what's important and what isn't. One practical way to do this is by integrating regular check-ins focused on prioritization. During these meetings, encourage team members to talk openly about what they're working on, and together identify the most impactful tasks. Help them apply the Breakthrough Blocker Test—asking whether a task truly moves the needle or if it's simply noise. This exercise helps them focus their energy, leading to more meaningful contributions.

Another key element of guiding your team is leading by example. Your actions set the standard for what is expected. If you make prioritization visible—if you openly discuss what you're choosing to focus on and why—you create a culture where strategic focus becomes the norm. Your behavior will serve as a guidepost, and over time, your team will start to internalize these principles, leading to increased productivity and satisfaction for everyone involved.

Creating a Culture of Focused Excellence in Your Organization

To build a culture of focused excellence, you need more than just individual actions—you need an environment that supports and encourages the behaviors you want to see. This kind of culture starts with your values and is reinforced by everything from the way meetings are run to how successes are celebrated. The goal is to create a space where everyone understands that focusing on what truly matters isn't just encouraged—it's expected.

Start by setting clear expectations. Make it known that in your organization, quality outweighs quantity. Emphasize that it's not about doing everything but about doing the right things well. This message needs to be consistent, not just in words but in actions. For instance, look at how projects are managed—are team members being pulled in ten different directions, or are they given the time and space to focus deeply on what matters most? The latter fosters focused excellence, the former leads to burnout and mediocrity.

Recognition also plays a powerful role in shaping culture. When you celebrate team wins, focus on how they were achieved, not just the results. Highlight how someone chose to eliminate unnecessary distractions to deliver high-quality work on a crucial project. By tying recognition to strategic focus and prioritization, you reinforce those values within the team.

Policies and practices can further cement this culture. Consider revising performance metrics to emphasize strategic impact rather than volume of tasks completed. For example, measure success by outcomes achieved, improvements in efficiency, or even contributions to team growth, rather than just hours logged or tasks ticked off. The more you align every aspect of your team's experience with the principles of focused excellence, the more ingrained these habits become.

Developing Tools for Team Growth and Accountability

For a culture of focused excellence to thrive, accountability must be integrated into your team's everyday processes. Accountability doesn't mean micromanaging—it means creating a system where team members feel responsible for their own progress and for contributing to the collective success.

Introduce shared tools that foster both growth and accountability. Task boards, shared action plans, and collaborative prioritization lists can be highly effective. These tools allow team members to see what others are focusing on, create opportunities for peer feedback, and ensure that everyone's efforts are aligned with the overall goals of the team. It's about transparency—everyone knowing who is working on what, and understanding how each task contributes to the larger picture.

Additionally, encourage peer support systems. Accountability doesn't have to be top-down; it can also be lateral. When team members feel comfortable discussing their priorities with one another, they hold each other to the commitments they've made. This fosters a sense of collective responsibility, which is crucial for maintaining high standards of focus and performance.

Regular one-on-one meetings can also be powerful. Use these check-ins not only to monitor progress but to talk about obstacles. If a team member is struggling with prioritization, this is your chance to coach them through it, to help refine their approach so they can contribute meaningfully. By showing genuine interest in their development, you're creating an environment where everyone feels supported in striving for excellence.

The Role of Emotional Intelligence in Breakthrough Leadership

Emotional intelligence (EI) is the cornerstone of effective leadership, especially when your goal is to inspire breakthroughs. Moving beyond personal performance to become a leader means you're responsible not only for the work being done but also for the wellbeing and motivation of your team.

Start by honing your self-awareness and empathy. Self-awareness allows you to understand how your actions and emotions affect the people around you, while empathy helps you connect with others on a meaningful level. These aren't soft skills; they are the building blocks of effective leadership. When your team members feel seen, heard, and valued, they're more likely to take risks, to strive for breakthroughs, and to trust you as their leader.

Being emotionally intelligent also means being adept at managing relationships within the team. Whether it's resolving conflicts, understanding different perspectives, or navigating team dynamics, the ability to read and respond appropriately to emotional cues is what sets apart effective leaders from the rest. Make it a habit to ask questions like, "How are you feeling about this project?" or "What can I do to support you better?" These questions may seem simple, but they open the door for honest communication and show your team that you value their emotional wellbeing as much as their output.

Emotional intelligence extends to managing your own stress and maintaining your resilience. Leadership can be draining, especially when you're guiding others through difficult times or working to maintain focus amid numerous distractions. Showing vulnerability—admitting when you need help, or when you don't have all the answers—can be powerful. It humanizes you and encourages your team members to do the same, fostering a culture of trust and mutual support.

Building a Shared Vision of Success

A breakthrough-driven leader is more than just a manager of tasks; they are a steward of vision. Your ability to articulate and rally your team around a shared vision can make all the difference in whether or not breakthroughs happen. A shared vision provides direction, motivation, and a sense of purpose—it is the "why" behind every action taken.

To build this vision, engage your team in its creation. Rather than presenting a fully-formed plan, start conversations about what success looks like for the team. Ask questions like, "What do we want to achieve together?" and "How can our work make a bigger impact?" These discussions aren't just about the end result; they're about ownership. When team members have a voice in shaping the vision, they're far more committed to achieving it.

Keep the vision visible. Remind your team regularly of what you're all working towards, and celebrate progress. A shared vision isn't static—it evolves with your team's achievements and changing circumstances. By keeping it dynamic and open to contributions, you ensure it remains relevant and inspiring. It's this constant engagement that turns a vision from an abstract idea into a powerful motivator that guides daily work.

Breakthrough-driven leadership is about more than just getting people to follow instructions; it's about inspiring a collective belief in the possibilities ahead. When you foster a shared vision, you're not just leading a team—you're empowering people to become leaders in their own right, each contributing uniquely to the broader mission.

Closing Thoughts: From Individual to Collective Breakthroughs

Becoming a breakthrough-driven leader is not about stepping away from what made you successful as an individual. It's about leveraging that success in new ways, using your focus, clarity, and determination to lift others. You're not abandoning personal achievements—you're multiplying them by creating the conditions for others to experience similar growth.

This chapter is about more than just leadership skills; it's about reimagining what success looks like. As you help others prioritize, guide them towards breakthroughs, and create a culture of focused excellence, your role evolves from individual high-achiever to transformational leader. You're setting the stage for collective success, where everyone's efforts are aligned and amplified, leading to breakthroughs that no one person could achieve alone.

Work–Life Balance...

The journey continues as we look at how to integrate these principles into the complexities of modern careers. The next chapter will explore how to navigate the challenges of managing multiple roles and projects, and how to apply breakthrough thinking even in the most demanding situations.

Chapter Fourteen

Breakthrough Balance: Integrating Work and Life

True breakthroughs are about more than just career success—they're about balance.

In the pursuit of our biggest goals, it's easy to get caught up in the idea that career success is the ultimate measure of achievement. But there's something deeper that we all crave: a sense of true fulfillment that goes beyond the office, beyond accolades, and into the fabric of our everyday lives. In this chapter, we're going to discover how to balance ambition with life satisfaction—using the CLEAR framework as our guide. By exploring how to integrate work and life in a meaningful way, you'll learn that true breakthroughs aren't just about climbing the ladder but enjoying the view along the way.

The key to satisfaction is knowing how to align work with life.

Applying CLEAR Principles to Personal Life and Relationships

Imagine having a simple framework that works for both your career and your life. The CLEAR framework isn't just for achieving breakthroughs at work—it can transform how you approach everything that matters to you, from your closest relationships to your health and personal happiness. In this section, we're going to explore how each step of the CLEAR method applies to different areas of your personal life, making balance not only achievable but sustainable.

- **Categorize**: Just as with your professional tasks, categorizing your personal priorities helps you understand where to focus your time and energy. Think of all the areas of your life that matter—family, friends, health, hobbies, personal growth. What are the core elements that truly fulfill you? Categorizing them allows you to see what's essential and what's taking up space without providing real value.

- **List Priorities**: After you've categorized, it's time to identify your key priorities. Maybe you've realized that nurturing your relationship with your partner is top of the list, or that focusing on your health is the foundation for everything else. Listing your priorities means being honest about what brings joy and fulfilment, even if it means reshuffling what's typically expected of you. It's about aligning your actions with what matters most.

- **Eliminate**: This is where things can get a little uncomfortable. Just as in your career, eliminating non-essential tasks in your personal life is crucial for balance. Think about the social obligations that drain you or the activities that you feel you "should" do but don't bring you real satisfaction. Imagine how freeing it would feel to say no to those things and free up space for what actually enriches your life.

- **Act**: Once you know what to prioritize and what to let go, it's time to act. This means dedicating time, energy, and attention to those priorities consistently. If you've chosen your health, commit to daily walks, or if it's family time, set aside evenings without distractions. Acting on these decisions regularly turns intention into reality.

- **Refine**: Life changes, and so do our priorities. Refining means regularly checking in with yourself to see if what you're focusing on is still working for you. Are you feeling more balanced? Has something shifted that requires a change in approach? Refining your actions keeps you from becoming stagnant and ensures that your path continues to serve your sense of fulfilment.

By applying CLEAR principles to your personal life, you'll notice that the same structure that helps you professionally can also bring clarity and peace to your home, relationships, and well-being.

True balance comes from aligning your intentions with your everyday actions.

Strategies for Maintaining Work-Life Harmony While Pursuing Ambitious Goals

Is it really possible to be ambitious and still maintain work-life harmony? The answer is yes, but it takes conscious planning and consistent reflection. In this section, we'll explore practical strategies for managing your time and energy so that you don't have to sacrifice one part of your life to succeed in another. It's about creating a lifestyle that supports your goals—not just in your career but in every aspect of your life.

1. **Set Boundaries Clearly and Early**: Boundaries are key to maintaining balance. If you set a rule that family dinners are non-negotiable, you need to communicate that to your work team and protect that time. Establishing these boundaries early on creates clear expectations, allowing you to protect your personal time without guilt.

2. **Schedule "Non-Negotiables"**: Just as you schedule important meetings, you need to schedule personal non-negotiables. This could be a workout, a date night, or simply time for reading and relaxing. By putting these things in your calendar, you treat them with the same importance as work-related commitments—because they are.

3. **Time Blocking for Balance**: Time blocking is one of the most effective ways to maintain balance. Designate blocks of time for different aspects of your life—work, health,

family, personal development. When you commit time to each area, it ensures that nothing gets neglected. It's about making sure that each part of your life gets its moment in the spotlight.

4. **Learn to Say No**: This is where elimination comes into play again. Saying no to additional projects, social events, or even unnecessary work tasks is about protecting your time for the things that really matter. When you say no to one thing, you're actually saying yes to something more meaningful.

5. **Embrace Imperfection**: One of the biggest traps for ambitious people is the pursuit of perfection—at work, at home, in relationships. But striving for balance doesn't mean being perfect in every area all the time. It's okay if sometimes work demands more, and it's okay if other times family takes precedence. Accepting that balance is dynamic and not always perfectly distributed is key to maintaining it long-term.

By applying these strategies, you'll be able to create a lifestyle that not only accommodates your ambitions but also enriches your personal life.

Balance is not about equal time—it's about equal meaning.

Redefining Success Beyond Career Achievements

What does success really mean to you? If success only means a high salary or a prestigious title, you may find yourself feeling unfulfilled even after achieving your career goals. This section is about expanding your definition of success to include the non-tangible aspects of life—those moments that are harder to measure but deeply important to our sense of well-being.

- **Emotional Fulfilment**: Success isn't just about material gain; it's about emotional well-being. How often do you feel happy, content, or at peace? Taking time to nurture emotional fulfilment means engaging in activities that make you feel alive—whether it's spending time with loved ones, pursuing a hobby, or simply relaxing in nature.

- **Strong Relationships**: There's no real success without strong, supportive relationships. Whether it's family, friends, or your community, the people around you play a huge role in how successful you feel. Investing in these relationships, being there for people who matter, and letting them support you when needed is crucial to a full sense of success.

- **Personal Growth and Learning**: Growth is an ongoing process. When we think of career success, we often focus on skills and achievements that have a direct benefit to our professional lives. But what about personal growth? This could be learning how to cook, practicing a new language, or gaining a better understanding of yourself. Success means constantly learning and growing, not just professionally, but personally.

- **Well-being and Health**: A successful life includes caring for your body and mind. When we chase career goals without caring for our health, we often find ourselves burnt out. Success means making well-being a priority—getting enough sleep, eating nourishing foods, and keeping your body active. Physical and mental health is what allows you to enjoy everything else you're working towards.

- **Purpose and Contribution**: True success comes when you align your career with a sense of purpose. It could be creating positive change in your workplace, helping others through your talents, or simply knowing that your actions make a difference. Contributing to something bigger than yourself is a powerful component of feeling successful.

When you redefine success to include these dimensions, your life becomes richer and more balanced. You're no longer solely focused on the next promotion but on building a life that feels deeply satisfying in every possible way.

True success is a life where every part contributes to a sense of purpose.

Conclusion: Creating a Life Worth Living

Integrating work and life isn't just a catchy concept—it's a necessity for a fulfilled existence. Through this chapter, we've explored how the CLEAR framework can bring focus not only to your career but to the very fabric of your personal life. We've looked at how prioritizing, eliminating non-essentials, and refining your approach can help create harmony between your ambitions and the relationships and experiences that bring you joy. You've learned practical tools for setting boundaries, protecting your non-negotiables, and redefining success on your own terms.

Balance isn't about achieving perfect equilibrium every day—it's about knowing what matters most and ensuring that those things are present in your life. It's about aligning your work, your relationships, your health, and your aspirations in a way that supports who you truly are and the life you truly want to lead. With each element of the CLEAR framework, you take steps toward a life that is not just about success, but about true, meaningful satisfaction.

An Even Bigger Stage...

Now that you've embraced balance as an essential part of breakthroughs, it's time to take those principles to an even bigger stage. In the next chapter, we will explore how you can extend your impact beyond your personal world and lead others to achieve their own breakthroughs—transforming your success into a force for collective change.

Chapter Fifteen

The Perpetual Breakthrough Mindset

Long-term success doesn't happen by accident; it's cultivated through intentional habits.

In today's fast-paced world, it's easy to achieve one breakthrough and then find yourself stagnating, waiting for the next big idea to somehow emerge. But true growth is about maintaining a mindset that continually fuels progress—no matter the circumstances. This chapter will guide you through practical strategies to establish a perpetual breakthrough mindset, so you can keep striving forward, even when things get tough. With the right habits and systems in place, you can create a career that's defined by continuous breakthroughs and lasting success.

The tools you'll learn here are not just quick fixes—they're lifestyle changes that will help you keep achieving, growing, and overcoming the inevitable plateaus that come with any ambitious journey.

Cultivating a Lifelong Commitment to Focused Growth

Growth is not a destination; it's a lifelong process that demands intention.

The first key to adopting a perpetual breakthrough mindset is cultivating a lifelong commitment to focused growth. This means that breakthroughs should never be seen as the endpoint. They are not goals that you check off a list and forget about. Instead, they're milestones on a longer journey. To consistently evolve, you need to commit to growth as a fundamental value in your professional life—an attitude that becomes part of who you are.

One of the best ways to do this is by developing a personal growth system. Think of it like tending a garden. You don't just plant seeds, walk away, and come back months later expecting a full bloom. You nurture the soil, water the plants, and remove the weeds. Growth in your career works the same way. It involves establishing routines that ensure you keep pushing forward and learning from every experience, even from failure.

A personal growth system could include regularly revisiting your goals, reading industry-related books or articles, seeking new experiences, or even engaging in mentoring—either as a mentor or a mentee. The idea is to keep yourself constantly challenged. You're not just chasing titles or achievements; you're cultivating a practice of ongoing improvement.

The mindset you choose today will shape your opportunities tomorrow.

Habits and Rituals for Sustaining the Breakthrough Mentality

Habits build the bridge between intention and action.

Breakthroughs don't come solely from working harder or staying busy. They arise when you implement consistent habits that channel your energy in the right direction. Sustaining a breakthrough mentality means embedding these habits into your daily routine so that your actions naturally align with your desire for growth.

One powerful habit is starting each day by focusing on your top priorities. This isn't about creating a to-do list that's twenty items long. Instead, focus on the one or two tasks that, if completed, will move you closer to your next breakthrough. By making this a morning ritual, you set the tone for the entire day. Your actions will be directed by intention rather than being swept away by the latest email or an unexpected request.

Another ritual involves a weekly reflection session. Spend an hour at the end of each week reviewing your wins, challenges, and the adjustments you need to make. It's like steering a ship—you need to periodically check your course, make corrections, and avoid the drift that comes when you're too caught up in daily routines. This habit helps you stay aligned with your larger vision.

You could also adopt what some call a "learning hour." Dedicate one hour a day, or at least a few times each week, to learning something new. It could be a podcast on industry trends, a tutorial on a new skill, or even a conversation with someone you admire. By making learning a ritual, you ensure that you're constantly evolving and that your mind remains open to fresh perspectives.

When habits become rituals, they take on a meaning beyond mere actions—they become an expression of your values.

Overcoming Plateaus and Reigniting Motivation

Every plateau presents an opportunity—if you know how to see it.

Hitting a plateau is one of the most common challenges faced by high achievers. After experiencing a breakthrough, it's natural to reach a point where progress feels stalled. This can be discouraging, especially if you're used to constant momentum. But plateaus are not necessarily a problem; they're a natural part of growth. The key is learning how to overcome them effectively and use them as a springboard to your next breakthrough.

The first strategy for overcoming plateaus is to reframe them as a period of consolidation. Think of a plateau not as stagnation, but as an opportunity to refine your skills, stabilize your progress, and prepare for the next leap forward. During these periods, it's important to double down on the fundamentals—fine-tune the skills you already have, and perfect what you've been working on.

Another effective approach is to reignite your motivation by setting micro-goals. These are small, achievable targets that inject a sense of accomplishment into your daily routine. Plateaus often occur because the excitement of achieving a major goal has worn off, and the next big goal seems far away. Micro-goals help bridge the gap, giving you the momentum to keep pushing forward.

Additionally, seek new sources of inspiration. Sometimes, plateaus happen because you've been focused on the same projects, the same people, or the same routines for too long. To break free, expose yourself to new environments—attend a conference, take on a new type of project, or connect with individuals outside your usual circle. Fresh experiences often reignite the fire you need to move past a stagnant phase.

Remember, plateaus are only temporary—if you keep moving, you'll eventually find yourself climbing again.

Creating a Growth-Oriented Environment

The company you keep and the space you occupy shape your potential.

An often-overlooked factor in sustaining a breakthrough mindset is the environment you create for yourself. Both your physical surroundings and the people you choose to engage with play a significant role in your ability to maintain focus, motivation, and growth.

Start with your physical workspace. A cluttered, distracting environment can make it difficult to concentrate on meaningful tasks. Designing a space that encourages focus—whether it's a quiet corner of your home, an organized office, or even a favorite café—can have a profound impact on your ability to maintain a growth-oriented mindset. Make sure your workspace is not only functional but also inspiring, filled with items that remind you of your goals or motivate you.

Beyond the physical environment, the people you surround yourself with are equally important. Are your friends, colleagues, and mentors encouraging you to grow? Surrounding yourself with individuals who challenge you and inspire you to push boundaries is a powerful way to maintain the breakthrough mentality. Engaging with a community of growth-oriented people provides emotional support and introduces you to new ideas and opportunities that you may not have discovered alone.

A growth environment is one that nudges you toward progress, even when motivation is fleeting.

The Power of Mentorship and Community

Guidance from others makes the journey less lonely and more rewarding.

Mentorship plays a critical role in sustaining growth. When you have someone who has navigated similar challenges and who's invested in your success, it can accelerate your progress and keep you focused during tough times. But mentorship isn't a one-way street—being a mentor is just as powerful for your growth. Teaching and guiding others forces you to articulate your beliefs, reflect on your experiences, and keep striving to set an example.

If you haven't yet sought out a mentor, now is the time. Mentors can offer insights that aren't easily available in books or courses. They bring a personal dimension to learning that helps you understand not just the "how" but also the "why" behind each step. Seek out someone you admire, whose career or personal growth journey resonates with you, and approach them with curiosity and a willingness to learn.

Conversely, take time to mentor others. It may seem like an added commitment when you're already stretched thin, but the act of teaching often sparks new insights into your own practices. It keeps you in a learning mindset and helps cement the principles of growth into your daily life.

Communities are also invaluable. Whether it's a group of colleagues who meet regularly to discuss challenges, an online community focused on your industry, or a group of friends committed to personal development, belonging to a community keeps you accountable. It also introduces you to a diversity of thoughts, which is crucial for preventing stagnation.

Growth is best cultivated in a community—people inspire and challenge each other to keep moving forward.

Revisiting and Evolving Your Goals

Your goals should evolve as you do, reflecting your new potential.

As you grow, it's crucial to revisit and refine your goals periodically. What seemed like an ambitious goal a year ago might now seem small, given your recent breakthroughs. Setting new, challenging goals keeps the fire burning and ensures you're continually striving for something greater.

The process of revisiting your goals should be deliberate. Schedule a quarterly or bi-annual review where you sit down and reflect on what you've achieved, what has changed, and what you want moving forward. Are your current goals still aligned with where you want to go? Do they still excite you? If not, it's time to evolve them.

Remember, growth isn't linear. There will be setbacks, periods of rapid advancement, and times of slower progress. The important thing is that your goals reflect your current level and push you just beyond it, into the space where real breakthroughs happen.

Your goals are a living entity—they grow as you do, adapting to who you are becoming.

Embracing Setbacks as Learning Opportunities

Failure is not the opposite of success—it is part of the path.

Setbacks are inevitable, and how you handle them will determine whether you maintain a breakthrough mindset. Too often, people see failures as a sign to give up or pivot to something entirely new. But in truth, every setback is rich with information—an opportunity to learn something critical that success would never have taught you.

To embrace setbacks effectively, practice reflection rather than rejection. Instead of pushing away the feelings of disappointment, ask yourself what led to the failure. What was within your control? What would you do differently next time? When you analyze failures with curiosity instead of judgment, they become an invaluable part of your growth toolkit.

A practical way to keep setbacks in perspective is to maintain a "failure journal." In this journal, record the setbacks you experience, how they made you feel, and what you learned from them. Over time, you'll begin to see that failure isn't something to be feared but something that often provides the richest material for your breakthroughs.

Growth doesn't happen in spite of setbacks—it happens because of them.

Cultivating Resilience Through Intentional Practice

Resilience is the muscle that keeps you moving when things get tough.

To sustain a breakthrough mindset, you need resilience—the capacity to recover quickly from difficulties and keep striving toward your goals. Resilience isn't something you either have or don't have. It's a skill that can be developed through intentional practice.

One powerful way to cultivate resilience is through mindfulness. This doesn't necessarily mean lengthy meditation sessions, although they can help. It can also be as simple as taking five minutes each day to sit quietly, breathe deeply, and remind yourself of your strengths. Practicing mindfulness helps you stay present during stressful moments, preventing your mind from spiraling into negative thoughts.

Physical exercise is another proven way to build resilience. When you challenge your body's limits, you're also training your mind to push past discomfort. It creates a natural resilience that translates well to other aspects of your life. Whether it's a run, a strength-training session, or a yoga practice, making exercise a non-negotiable part of your routine will help bolster your mental toughness.

The more you intentionally practice resilience, the stronger your breakthrough mindset becomes.

Celebrating Your Wins—Big and Small

Acknowledging progress fuels future progress.

To maintain a perpetual breakthrough mindset, it's essential to celebrate your wins—both big and small. Many high achievers are quick to move on to the next goal without fully acknowledging what they've already accomplished. While ambition is valuable, it's equally important to pause and appreciate your achievements.

Celebrating wins doesn't have to be elaborate. It could be as simple as treating yourself to your favorite coffee after completing a challenging project or taking a day off to relax and recharge. The important part is that you recognize the effort you've put in and the progress you've made.

Keeping a "win log" is a powerful way to track and celebrate your successes. Each time you achieve something, no matter how small, write it down. Over time, this log becomes a tangible reminder of your journey and the breakthroughs you've achieved along the way. It helps maintain motivation and keeps you focused on what's possible.

Celebrating your wins isn't self-indulgent—it's a necessary part of sustaining your growth journey.

Beyond Personal Triumph...

As you embrace the perpetual breakthrough mindset, you become not only a catalyst for your own growth but also

an inspiration for others. In the next chapter, we will explore how to extend your breakthrough impact beyond your personal goals and begin to influence your industry, shaping the future of work and driving meaningful change. Let's explore how you can become an industry catalyst and leverage your newfound clarity to lead with purpose and innovation.

"Success is not the key to happiness.
Happiness is the key to success.
If you love what you are doing, you will be successful."
- Albert Schweitzer

Chapter Sixteen

Breakthrough Influence: Becoming an Industry Catalyst

What if your breakthrough could ignite an entire industry?

Your success story doesn't have to end with personal triumph. Once you've mastered the art of focused prioritization and achieved breakthrough results in your own career, it's time to leverage that clarity to transform the world around you. In this chapter, we'll explore how you can extend your influence, becoming not just an achiever, but a catalyst for innovation in your field—someone who inspires change and drives progress on a larger scale. With actionable strategies for thought leadership, professional networking, and contributing to industry-wide shifts, this is your chance to make a broader impact.

By turning personal breakthroughs into collective inspiration, you can redefine the boundaries of your influence.

Leveraging Newfound Clarity to Drive Industry Innovation

You've done the work to get clear on what matters most. Now, it's time to think about how that clarity can spark change beyond your own sphere of influence. **Your ability to simplify, prioritize, and execute is an asset that can reshape not only your career but also the way others perceive and solve problems in your industry.** Imagine if everyone in your field had the same razor-sharp focus on what truly matters—the kind of focus that drives real, tangible results.

One of the most effective ways to leverage this clarity is by identifying the gaps and opportunities that others might be missing. With your honed sense of what's important, you're uniquely positioned to notice inefficiencies or challenges that could use innovative solutions. **Think of yourself as a bridge—the person who connects what currently exists with what could be.** Use your insights to propose new systems, approaches, or ideas. This isn't about grand gestures; it's about finding small but meaningful changes that can have a big impact.

For example, consider the leaders in tech who didn't invent completely new technologies but instead found better ways to make them accessible. The real value lies in how you help others see a new possibility—transforming confusion into clarity and hesitancy into action. **Becoming an industry catalyst is about seeing the bigger picture and acting in a way that benefits not just you but everyone around you.**

Strategies for Thought Leadership and Professional Networking

True influence in your industry doesn't happen overnight; it's built on relationships, reputation, and resonance. Thought leadership is more than just a buzzword—it's about leading conversations, challenging norms, and sharing ideas that push your field forward. You've already learned to identify what matters most for your own success; now it's time to help others understand what should matter for theirs.

One of the first steps to becoming a thought leader is sharing your journey openly. This means being transparent about your failures as much as your successes. **When you share the challenges you faced, and how you overcame them, you build credibility and relatability.** People are more likely to be inspired by someone who has not only succeeded but also stumbled along the way and gotten back up. This authenticity is what sets genuine thought leaders apart from those who merely want the title.

Consider starting small. Write articles or blog posts about lessons you've learned, share insights on social media, or offer to speak at industry events. It's not about being the loudest voice in the room but about consistently providing value. **Every time you share an insight, you help build a more focused and effective industry.** Moreover, leveraging platforms like LinkedIn or Medium allows you to amplify your influence and connect directly with others who are on similar journeys.

Networking is a crucial component of extending your influence, but it shouldn't feel transactional. The goal is to build relationships that are genuine and mutually beneficial. Reach out to others in your field—not just the "experts" but also those who are at different stages of their journey. **Think of networking as an opportunity to learn and share, rather than just a way to get ahead.** Offer mentorship, participate in discussions, and be generous with your time when others reach out for advice. Authenticity and generosity in your interactions will naturally position you as a leader.

Creating Positive Change Beyond the Immediate Sphere

The influence you build as an industry catalyst shouldn't be limited to your immediate circle or the confines of your office walls. **The true measure of your success as a catalyst is the positive change you bring to your field as a whole.** It's about contributing to something larger than yourself—creating an environment where innovation, focus, and progress thrive.

One powerful way to achieve this is by nurturing a culture of learning and growth within your organization or community. This might mean creating opportunities for knowledge sharing, such as hosting workshops or informal meetups where colleagues can discuss the challenges they face and how they're overcoming them. **By fostering an environment where focused prioritization and selective ignorance are seen as valuable skills, you help shape the way others approach their work.**

Another aspect of creating positive change is advocating for systemic shifts that improve how your industry operates. This could involve pushing for more efficient processes, ethical standards, or advocating for changes that reduce unnecessary work and promote well-being. **The key is to use your influence to make the professional environment more conducive to breakthroughs, not just for yourself but for everyone.**

Lastly, remember that positive change often starts small. It's in the little things—helping a colleague prioritize better, suggesting a more streamlined process, or simply being a role model of what focused, effective work looks like. **Every small action contributes to a larger cultural shift.** Your role as an industry catalyst means that every focused, clear-headed decision you make sets an example that ripples outwards.

Building a Culture of Focused Excellence

Creating positive change within your industry also means helping shape a culture that values focused excellence. **Breakthroughs are not one-off events; they are the result of consistent, dedicated effort over time.** As an industry catalyst, your role includes inspiring this mindset in others and making it a part of your professional community's DNA.

Start by modelling what focused excellence looks like in your daily life. Show up consistently, make thoughtful decisions about where you invest your time, and celebrate the value of saying "no" to distractions. **People take cues from those they admire—your commitment to focused excellence will encourage others to reconsider how they work, too.** When others see the tangible benefits that come from prioritizing effectively, it creates a ripple effect that inspires change.

Beyond individual modelling, consider how you can institutionalize this culture. Maybe it's about proposing initiatives within your organization that reward thoughtful prioritization rather than busyness. **Consider encouraging the implementation of focus-driven workshops, where teams can reassess their goals and align on what truly matters.** Small systemic changes like these can have profound effects on the collective mindset, moving from the glorification of "being busy" to celebrating meaningful progress.

Inspiration doesn't always come from grand speeches or ambitious projects—sometimes, it's the small yet consistent actions that have the most impact. **Becoming an industry catalyst is about showing that focused, deliberate effort always beats scattered busyness.** By leading through example and advocating for a culture of focused excellence, you help set the stage for collective breakthroughs.

From Influence to Impact: Thought Leadership in Action

Influence is powerful, but impact is where true change happens. **As you work on building influence within your industry, the next step is transforming that influence into concrete action that moves the needle.** This is where you transition from sharing ideas to driving initiatives that make those ideas a reality.

One way to begin is by taking ownership of a problem you've identified in your industry. Whether it's an inefficiency, a lack of resources, or an overlooked opportunity, use your platform to initiate change. **This could involve leading a project, starting**

a collaborative group to brainstorm solutions, or partnering with others who share your vision. By turning influence into action, you demonstrate that thought leadership isn't just about ideas—it's about making real-world differences.

Another way to create impact is by championing underrepresented voices in your industry. Sometimes, the most groundbreaking ideas come from those who are often overlooked. **Use your position to advocate for those who may not have the same platform but have something valuable to contribute.** Helping amplify diverse perspectives not only strengthens the fabric of your industry but also encourages a culture where the best ideas, regardless of where they come from, rise to the top.

The key to transitioning from influence to impact lies in consistency. You've already mastered consistency in your personal habits—now apply that same dedication to how you contribute to the larger ecosystem. **By taking intentional steps toward making a tangible impact, you ensure that your influence leaves a lasting mark on your industry.**

Making Breakthroughs Last

As you continue to expand your influence, it's crucial to ensure that the breakthroughs you facilitate—both for yourself and others—are sustainable. **This means focusing on not just immediate wins but also long-term progress that benefits your industry over time.** Breakthrough influence isn't just about making a splash; it's about creating ripples that last.

One way to make breakthroughs lasting is to build systems that outlive your direct involvement. **For instance, develop best**

practices that can be shared and implemented even after you've moved on to another project or role. Documentation, training resources, and knowledge-sharing platforms are key tools that ensure the processes you've optimized and the innovations you've championed can continue to thrive.

Also, consider mentoring others to carry forward the work you've started. **By identifying and nurturing future leaders within your organization or network, you create a pipeline of change agents who can continue to drive positive outcomes.** Your influence becomes exponential when you empower others to take up the mantle and continue the work of prioritizing, focusing, and innovating.

Breakthroughs are a reflection of mindset as much as they are about tactics. **Cultivate a mindset of constant learning and adaptability, both in yourself and in those around you.** The more you can foster a culture that values curiosity and openness to change, the more resilient your industry will become in the face of future challenges.

Building on Your Influence...

By the end of this chapter, you should be feeling empowered not only to lead yourself but to lead others toward breakthroughs. **The next step is to explore how you can apply these principles to tackle the complexities of career pivots and major transitions, ensuring that no matter what path you choose, your influence continues to grow.**

Let's dive into how you can use your newfound clarity and influence to confidently navigate significant changes—turning career shifts into opportunities for further growth and impact.

"Racing is a matter of spirit, not strength."
- Janet Guthrie
(First woman to compete in the Indianapolis 500)

Chapter Seventeen

Mastering Career Pivots and Transitions

Career pivots are not moments of chaos but opportunities for deliberate reinvention.

Too often, when faced with a career change, we see it as a daunting crisis rather than a powerful opportunity to realign our professional lives with our true aspirations. These transitions, though uncertain, can be the key to unlocking more fulfilling work and a deeper sense of purpose. In this chapter, we'll explore how to harness the **Breakthrough Blocker Method** to navigate these changes with intention, clarity, and confidence, transforming them into meaningful moments of growth.

When you understand how to take charge of career transitions, uncertainty becomes your ally.

Applying the Breakthrough Blocker Method to Career Changes

A career pivot often feels like standing at a crossroads, staring at multiple diverging paths. The fear of making the wrong decision can be paralyzing, but that's where the **Breakthrough Blocker Method** steps in, turning confusion into clarity. When you apply this method to a career pivot, it allows you to break down a seemingly overwhelming change into actionable, manageable steps.

The **CLEAR framework** is an excellent guide for these moments. Each part of the framework—**Categorize, List, Eliminate, Act, Refine**—is a compass that directs your decisions at pivotal junctures. Imagine standing at the precipice of a new career decision. Instead of panicking about the unknowns, you methodically categorize your options, assess your true priorities, eliminate distractions, and take actionable steps to align with your long-term goals. For instance, categorizing your current skills and experiences can help you identify where you can create the most significant impact. From there, listing your top priorities makes it clear which opportunities align with your goals and which are mere distractions.

The **Eliminate** step is particularly vital during career pivots. It involves letting go of outdated goals, unnecessary commitments, and even habits that may have once served you but are now holding you back. Sometimes, it also means parting ways with the perceived security of your current position—a leap that can feel intimidating but is often necessary for genuine growth. The **Breakthrough Blocker Method** helps ensure that your choices are deliberate, allowing you to ignore the noise and focus on what will drive your career forward.

A structured approach can transform a pivot from a reactive move into a proactive, empowering choice.

Identifying and Seizing Transformative Opportunities

Career changes are more than just shifts in job titles or companies; they're opportunities to transform your professional trajectory entirely. The most successful people see these transitions not as risks but as opportunities—moments when they can redefine their contributions and align more closely with their true calling. But how do you learn to identify these moments, especially when the chaos of change blurs your vision?

One of the most effective strategies is to reframe uncertainty as a natural part of progress. Opportunities for transformation often come disguised as challenges—perhaps a restructuring at work, an unexpected job loss, or the realization that your current path no longer excites you. Instead of focusing on the discomfort, you can focus on the underlying opportunity: a chance to reimagine what success looks like for you.

The CLEAR framework offers a systematic way to assess these moments. During a time of upheaval, the **Categorize** phase can help you sift through all the possibilities before you. Should you move industries? Seek a different role within your current field? Start your own venture? The key here is not to rush decisions but to categorize all your options by evaluating their alignment with your personal and professional aspirations.

After categorizing, it's essential to **List** and **prioritize**. This step helps you determine which opportunities are genuinely transformative and which ones simply offer temporary relief. It's easy to take the first opportunity that presents itself, especially when uncertainty looms large. However, by listing and weighing these options, you avoid settling and instead identify paths that will genuinely move you toward a breakthrough.

Finally, **Act** on the insights you've gained—take calculated, deliberate steps towards the opportunity that aligns best with your goals. This doesn't necessarily mean dramatic actions all at once; it might begin with taking a course, expanding your network in a new field, or even committing to learn more about an area that excites you. The power of the **Breakthrough Blocker Method** lies in its ability to turn the overwhelming process of change into a deliberate journey of growth.

The key to seizing opportunities is in recognizing that transformation is always on the other side of discomfort.

Navigating Uncertainty with Clarity and Purpose

Career transitions are often synonymous with uncertainty—the very thing many people spend their lives trying to avoid. However, the truth is, uncertainty is unavoidable, especially when you are making moves that are bold and meaningful. The difference between those who thrive during a career pivot and those who struggle is not the absence of uncertainty, but their ability to embrace it with clarity and purpose.

Mental clarity is crucial during these times. A cluttered mind tends to focus on fear—fear of the unknown, fear of failure, fear of making the wrong choice. To navigate career pivots successfully, you need strategies to maintain a clear and focused mindset. The **Breakthrough Blocker Method** helps you cut through this mental clutter by focusing only on the decisions that truly matter. Eliminating non-essential tasks, roles, and even thought patterns that cause unnecessary worry can create the mental space required for clear decision-making.

In this context, the **Refine** aspect of the CLEAR framework becomes vital. Refinement is about continually evaluating your progress and making adjustments along the way. It is easy to assume that the end goal of a career pivot is to land a new role or start a new business. But the truth is, every career change is a continuous process of growth and realignment. What felt like the perfect next step six months ago may need adjustment as you gain more clarity and experience. Refinement keeps you adaptable, allowing you to pivot yet again when necessary—not out of panic, but out of deliberate choice.

One practical way to ensure you maintain clarity during uncertainty is to establish **guiding principles** for your career. These are non-negotiables—core values that will inform your decisions no matter how uncertain things get. For example, if one of your guiding principles is to work in a role that supports creativity and autonomy, any career opportunity that doesn't align with this value can be eliminated early in the decision-making process. This kind of clarity reduces the number of decisions you need to make, helping you focus only on the options that are genuinely viable.

Uncertainty, when embraced with purpose, is the birthplace of all career breakthroughs.

From Hesitation to Empowered Action

Career pivots often begin with hesitation. The fear of the unknown, the loss of identity, and the challenge of starting over can create a sense of inertia that feels impossible to overcome. But what if that hesitation was simply an invitation to evaluate, rethink, and ultimately empower yourself to take action that aligns with who you truly are?

The **Breakthrough Blocker Method** transforms hesitation into empowered action by giving you a roadmap that doesn't ignore your fears but addresses them head-on. The **Categorize** step helps you put your fears into context—understanding what's holding you back and whether those fears are based on reality or assumptions. This step can involve a deep dive into your anxieties, breaking them down into specific, understandable pieces. For example, you might fear financial instability during a career change. Categorizing that fear allows you to see what part of it is realistic and what part is an overgeneralization.

The **List** phase then becomes about writing down actionable steps to address each fear. For instance, if a fear is lack of knowledge in a new industry, one action might be to find a mentor who has successfully navigated a similar transition. You might also list steps like attending industry workshops, taking relevant online courses, or even conducting informational interviews with people already in that field. The point is to turn the abstract nature of fear into concrete, doable actions that guide you forward.

Eliminate becomes your tool to discard unproductive fears and false beliefs that hinder your progress. Fear of failure is often grounded in the misconception that a failed attempt means starting from scratch, but every "failure" in a career pivot is an opportunity to learn, grow, and refine your direction. It's about recognizing that failure isn't a stopping point—it's a critical checkpoint that provides data on what worked and what didn't. Eliminating these misconceptions allows you to move with less emotional baggage, opening up new pathways that were previously obscured by self-doubt.

Finally, the **Act** step turns all the introspection into movement. Taking empowered action means making decisions that reflect your values and your aspirations, rather than succumbing to external pressures or internal doubts. Action might start small—such as setting up a weekly goal related to your career shift—but it's this consistent movement that builds momentum. Empowerment doesn't necessarily come from eliminating fear—it comes from moving forward despite it, with a clear vision of what you want to achieve. Each action you take chips away at hesitation, building a foundation of courage that only strengthens with time.

One way to foster a mindset of empowered action is to celebrate small wins. Each step you take, however minor it might seem, is progress. Whether it's reaching out to a mentor, enrolling in a new class, or simply drafting a plan, every action deserves acknowledgment. These small wins accumulate and reinforce the sense that you are capable of navigating this transition.

The journey from hesitation to empowered action is about transforming fear into a series of deliberate, courageous choices. When you break down the fear, list concrete steps, eliminate limiting beliefs, and take action, you transform hesitation into the power to move forward with purpose.

Reinventing Yourself While Honoring Your Past

One of the biggest challenges during a career pivot is reconciling your past identity with your future aspirations. You may wonder how to leave behind what you once worked so hard to achieve, without feeling like those years were wasted. The key lies in recognizing that every experience has value, even if its role in your future isn't immediately obvious. Every job, project, or role you've held has helped shape your skills, perspectives, and resilience. These experiences are the raw material that can fuel your future success, even if the final product looks very different from what you initially imagined.

When applying the **CLEAR framework** during a career transition, **Categorizing** your past experiences is crucial. Instead of viewing your previous roles as irrelevant to your new aspirations, think of each one as a part of a toolkit you carry into the future. Perhaps you're moving from a corporate role to a creative one—the project management skills, discipline, and team leadership from your corporate experience are incredibly valuable, even if the industry is different. Additionally, those same skills might allow you to bring a unique perspective to your new creative endeavors, helping you stand out in a competitive field.

Categorizing also involves recognizing which aspects of your past still align with your future aspirations. Maybe you've always thrived in environments that require a lot of structure, and now you're moving to an industry that seems more fluid and uncertain. Understanding which elements of your past experience can provide stability, and which might need adjustment, can make the transition far smoother.

Listing these transferable skills not only helps you see the value in your past but also provides clarity about what you can offer in your next role. By acknowledging the skills that have served you well and the ones that may no longer be necessary, you can reinvent yourself while staying true to the core experiences that make you unique. For example, you might have excellent skills in data analysis that aren't directly applicable to your new creative role, but the analytical mindset can still be a valuable asset, helping you solve problems or strategize more effectively.

Moreover, listing your skills helps in crafting your narrative when talking to potential employers or collaborators. It's not just about knowing what you can do but about effectively communicating how your past adds value to your future pursuits. This list can also serve as a reminder during moments of doubt, reinforcing the idea that your past efforts weren't wasted but are building blocks for what's next.

During the **Eliminate** phase, it's important to let go of the parts of your past identity that no longer serve you. Maybe you defined yourself by a specific job title, or perhaps your sense of worth was tied to the prestige of your previous company. Letting go of these attachments is not easy, but it's necessary for genuine reinvention. Remember, you're not discarding your past; you're making space for your next evolution. This process might mean letting go of rigid ideas about what success looks like, particularly if your new path is unconventional. It can be freeing to redefine success on your own terms—terms that resonate with where you are now and where you wish to go.

Elimination also involves discarding mindsets that limit growth. If you've held beliefs like "I'm only good at one thing" or "I can't learn something entirely new at this stage of my career," it's time to let them go. These limiting beliefs are often more obstructive than external obstacles, and eliminating them creates the mental freedom needed to explore new opportunities without the baggage of self-imposed limits.

Finally, think of **Reinvention** as an ongoing process. It doesn't mean erasing who you were—it means building upon it with intention and vision. Reinvention is dynamic; it allows you to layer new skills, interests, and experiences on top of what you already have. It means recognizing that the best way to honor your past is not to let it dictate your future but to use it as a springboard to propel yourself forward. Reinvention means having the courage to evolve and the wisdom to understand that your past is a valuable ally in that evolution.

Embrace your past as the foundation of who you are becoming. Reinventing yourself doesn't mean disowning the previous chapters of your story; it means transforming them into an asset—a rich collection of experiences and skills that bring depth and character to whatever you choose to do next. This approach will not only help you transition more effectively but will also make your future endeavors far more rewarding, as they'll be infused with the authenticity that comes from honoring the journey that brought you here.

Reinvention doesn't mean erasing who you were—it means building upon it with intention, vision, and a clear understanding of the value of your past experiences.

Building a Network to Support Your Transition

Career pivots are not just about individual action—they're about surrounding yourself with the right support. Whether you're switching fields, starting something entirely new, or stepping into leadership, your network plays a vital role in providing insight, encouragement, and opportunities. A common misconception is that networks are purely transactional—an exchange of favors or connections. However, during a career pivot, a genuine support network is about building relationships that add mutual value.

Categorizing your network is a practical first step in understanding who can help you during your transition. Identify mentors, peers, industry contacts, and even friends who can offer different types of support—emotional, informational, and strategic. Not every contact in your network will be relevant for your new path, and that's okay. By categorizing them, you understand who to reach out to and for what kind of guidance.

Once you've **Listed** your key contacts, it's time to **Act**. Reach out, reconnect, and clearly communicate your career aspirations. Let them know where you're headed and how they might help, whether that's through advice, connections, or simply sharing their own experiences of change. People are more willing to help than you might think, especially when you're clear about what you need.

Eliminating fears around asking for help is also crucial here. Many of us hold back from reaching out because we fear appearing vulnerable or unsure. However, career pivots are times when vulnerability becomes a strength—it shows you're open to growth and eager to learn. **Refining** your network involves nurturing those relationships over time, not just when you need something. Offer value to others, share your experiences, and stay connected. The more you refine your network, the more genuine it becomes—creating a web of support that will be there for every career change, not just the current one.

A well-nurtured network turns career pivots from solitary struggles into collective journeys of growth.

Thriving Amid Disruption

The journey of mastering career pivots isn't just about managing change—it's about actively thriving in the midst of it. As we look to the future, consider how the skills and insights gained from personal career transitions can be leveraged in a broader context. In the next chapter, we'll explore how to not only adapt to, but also excel in, an ever-changing professional world where disruption is the new norm.

Get ready to future-proof your career by turning every challenge into an opportunity for reinvention and growth.

"Success is simple. Do what's right, the right way, at the right time."
– Arnold H. Glasow

Chapter Eighteen

The Future of Work: Thriving in an Age of Disruption

The future of work is here, and it's evolving faster than ever.

We're seeing shifts driven by technology, changing values, and unpredictable global events—and staying ahead means adapting with clarity and purpose. This chapter is about navigating these shifts and preparing yourself to not just survive but thrive in a work environment that's increasingly complex and dynamic.

In the past, success often meant sticking to a set path—going to school, landing a good job, and climbing the corporate ladder. But today, that path looks more like a winding road with detours, unexpected bumps, and new destinations appearing on the horizon. If you're still trying to follow the old blueprint, you might be missing out on the opportunities that come with embracing uncertainty and disruption. By understanding how to position yourself for the future, you can turn the unpredictability of work into a powerful advantage.

In this chapter, we're going to cover three core strategies: anticipating and adapting to emerging career landscapes, leveraging technology while keeping human skills at the forefront, and positioning yourself for long-term success. Let's dive in and explore how to make the future of work, work for you.

Anticipating and Adapting to Emerging Career Landscapes

Change is constant, but today's career landscapes are shifting at an unprecedented pace. Understanding how these changes affect your industry is crucial if you want to stay relevant and competitive. The first step is to develop a radar for trends—both technological and cultural—so you can anticipate shifts before they become mainstream.

Take, for example, the rise of remote work. Just a few years ago, the idea of working from home was often considered a luxury or reserved for freelancers. Now, it's become an expectation for many professionals. Companies have had to adapt to this shift, and so have employees. Those who saw this trend coming and invested in building skills like virtual communication and self-management were better prepared when remote work suddenly became the norm.

But remote work is just the tip of the iceberg. Artificial intelligence (AI) is reshaping industries, automation is changing the skills that are in demand, and the gig economy is creating new opportunities for people to work on their own terms. The key is not to fear these changes but to adapt. Start by regularly scanning news sources, industry reports, and thought leadership articles to stay informed. This will help you identify emerging opportunities and prepare for them before others do.

Another critical aspect of anticipating change is embracing lifelong learning. The skills you have today may not be the ones you need tomorrow. Make it a habit to invest in your education—whether that means taking an online course, attending a workshop, or simply learning from colleagues. The goal is to stay flexible and always be ready to pivot when new opportunities arise.

To adapt to emerging career landscapes effectively, you also need to be proactive about networking. Connect with others in your field, attend industry events (even virtually), and engage in discussions about where your industry is headed. By doing so, you not only keep yourself informed but also position yourself as someone who's at the forefront of change—a quality that employers and collaborators will value.

Key Takeaway: The future belongs to those who anticipate change and adapt proactively. Stay informed, keep learning, and maintain a strong network to navigate shifting career landscapes.

Leveraging Technology While Maintaining a Human-Centric Focus

Technology is transforming how we work, but it's the human touch that makes the difference in how successful we are at adapting. As much as AI, automation, and digital tools are changing industries, the skills that set people apart are still very much human—things like creativity, emotional intelligence, and the ability to connect with others.

Take AI, for example. It can analyze data faster than any human, but it still needs people to interpret the results, make decisions, and apply insights in a meaningful way. That's why it's crucial to see technology as a tool that enhances your abilities rather than something that replaces them. By learning to work alongside technology, you can amplify your strengths and focus on the aspects of work that require human insight—like strategic thinking and building relationships.

Consider the role of empathy in leadership. As teams become more distributed, the ability to understand and connect with others has become even more important. Technology helps us stay in touch, but it's the human effort to truly listen, understand, and respond to the needs of our colleagues that keeps teams cohesive and motivated. Leaders who embrace both technology and humanity are the ones who will thrive in this new environment.

Another example is the use of automation tools to streamline repetitive tasks. Rather than seeing this as a threat, consider it an opportunity to free up time for work that's more meaningful. By automating parts of your workflow, you can focus on problem-solving, creativity, and strategic initiatives that truly add value to your career.

Maintaining a human-centric focus also means prioritizing well-being. As technology makes it easier to stay connected 24/7, the risk of burnout is real. Setting boundaries, practicing digital detoxes, and focusing on activities that foster mental health are more important than ever. Thriving in the future of work isn't just about keeping up with technology; it's also about ensuring you remain balanced, fulfilled, and connected to what matters most.

Key Takeaway: Use technology as an amplifier of your human skills—not a replacement. Balance the efficiency of tech tools with the irreplaceable value of empathy, creativity, and well-being.

Positioning Yourself for Long-Term Success in a Rapidly Changing World

Long-term success in a fast-evolving world requires a combination of adaptability, vision, and resilience. It's not just about reacting to changes as they happen, but about setting yourself up to thrive no matter what comes your way. This means cultivating a mindset that embraces uncertainty, prioritizes growth, and is always looking for the next opportunity to learn.

The first step is to develop what we can call a "future-proof skillset." These are skills that are likely to be valuable regardless of how technology or industries change. Think about competencies like critical thinking, communication, adaptability, and emotional intelligence. These skills don't go out of style because they're fundamentally about how you interact with the world and solve problems—something machines can't fully replicate.

Positioning yourself for long-term success also involves building a personal brand that reflects your expertise, adaptability, and vision. In a world where career paths are less linear, being known for what you do and how you do it can open doors to opportunities you might not have imagined. Your personal brand is the reputation that follows you—and in a time when people are changing jobs and industries more often, having a strong, positive reputation can be a major advantage.

One effective way to build your brand is by sharing your insights publicly. This could mean writing articles, posting on LinkedIn, speaking at conferences, or even starting a podcast. The key is to position yourself as a thought leader who's not just responding to trends but anticipating them and adding your unique perspective. It's about showing that you're engaged, informed, and proactive—qualities that are highly attractive to potential employers, clients, or collaborators.

Another key aspect of positioning yourself for the future is resilience. Disruptions—whether global or personal—are a part of life. The question isn't if you will face challenges, but how you will respond when they happen. Developing resilience means learning how to bounce back from setbacks, maintain perspective, and stay committed to your long-term goals even when circumstances change. It's about focusing on what you can control, letting go of what you can't, and continually moving forward.

Finally, always be on the lookout for growth opportunities. Whether it's a chance to take on a new role, learn a new skill, or step outside your comfort zone, long-term success is often about being willing to take calculated risks. Growth doesn't happen when you're comfortable; it happens when you challenge yourself and stretch your abilities. By adopting a growth mindset and actively seeking out ways to learn and improve, you're positioning yourself not just for survival, but for true success.

Key Takeaway: Position yourself for long-term success by cultivating a future-proof skillset, building a personal brand, embracing resilience, and always seeking opportunities for growth.

Looking Ahead: Shaping Your Own Future

The future of work is filled with possibilities, but it's up to you to shape your own path. By anticipating and adapting to changes, leveraging technology in a human-centric way, and positioning yourself with the right skills and mindset, you can thrive in a world that's constantly evolving. The tools, strategies, and mindsets discussed in this chapter aren't just about keeping up—they're about getting ahead and creating a career that's meaningful, fulfilling, and resilient to whatever the future holds.

As we move into the next chapter, we'll explore how you can take the breakthroughs you've achieved and use them to influence not just your career but your industry. It's time to look beyond personal growth and consider the broader impact you can make—let's discover how to become a catalyst for innovation and positive change in your professional community.

"You can't win the race by running at full speed the whole time. Smart pacing matters."

– Unknown

Chapter Nineteen

Conclusion: Your Breakthrough Legacy

Your journey to clarity and success has only just begun.

Throughout this book, you've learned how to navigate the overwhelming demands of modern professional life, discovered how to prioritize effectively, and implemented the Breakthrough Blocker Method to clear away the clutter that held you back. But as you reach the end of this book, it's important to remember that this is not the conclusion of your journey—it's just the beginning of a new chapter in your professional and personal life.

The transformative steps you've taken—identifying your blockers, implementing strategic ignorance, and setting clear priorities—have brought you to a place of new awareness and momentum. You now have a better grasp of where your time and energy are best invested, and you've seen firsthand the power of eliminating what doesn't serve you. This journey has prepared you to be the driver of your own success story, where focus and deliberate action are your greatest tools.

This chapter is all about reflection, celebration, and the anticipation of what comes next. We'll explore how your personal breakthroughs don't just end with you; instead, they have a ripple effect that can influence others, your organization, and even your industry. It's about stepping back, acknowledging the transformation you've undergone, and understanding the lasting impact of these changes. Now, let's dive in.

Reflect on Your Transformative Journey

Take a moment to reflect on how far you've come. It may seem like just yesterday that you were caught in the whirlwind of too many commitments and conflicting priorities. You might remember the constant tension of always feeling busy, but never truly making progress. Now, you've shifted from that reactive state to one of proactive control. You're leading your life with intention, rather than letting it lead you.

- **Acknowledge Your Growth**: Look back at where you started. In Chapter 1, we talked about the "Overwhelm Epidemic," a phenomenon affecting so many professionals today. At that point, you may have recognized your own story in the pages—the struggle to keep your head above water. But as you worked through the CLEAR framework, something changed. You began to make sense of the chaos.

- **From Chaos to Clarity**: Think about the work you've done in categorizing tasks, eliminating what didn't matter, and identifying the true priorities that align with your career goals. The fog has lifted. You have clarity now, and with clarity comes the power to make meaningful decisions about your time and energy.

- **Celebrate Your Wins**: It's also important to celebrate the wins—both big and small. Every moment you chose to prioritize your North Star goals over distractions, every task you courageously eliminated, and every focused action you took brought you here. Those small victories matter, and they add up to something transformative. Celebrate them, because they're the stepping stones of your breakthrough.

The Ripple Effect of Personal Breakthroughs on Your Career and Beyond

Your breakthrough journey is not just about you—it's about the people around you, too. When one person breaks free from the burden of overwhelm and starts to prioritize effectively, it creates ripples. These ripples extend to your team, your colleagues, and even your personal relationships.

- **Impact on Your Environment**: By embracing the Breakthrough Blocker Method, you've likely started to influence others without even realizing it. Your focus, clarity, and decisiveness set an example for those around you. Whether it's a co-worker noticing the efficiency in your workflow or a family member seeing how present you are during personal time, your actions have a way of inspiring change.

- **Leading Through Example**: The truth is, people are always watching—not in a judgmental way, but because we're wired to observe and learn from one another. When others see you break through the noise and thrive, they'll be curious. They'll want to know what changed, and they'll look to you for guidance. This is your opportunity to lead by example, showing others that it's not about doing more, but about doing what truly matters.

- **Inspiring Organizational Change**: Beyond individual influence, there's an opportunity to create broader change. In Chapter 13, we discussed becoming a breakthrough-driven leader—someone who inspires others to adopt focused prioritization strategies. As you continue to refine your approach, consider how these principles can foster a culture of clarity and intentionality within your organization. You're not just making a difference for yourself; you're paving the way for others to experience breakthroughs, too.

Invitation to Join the Community of Breakthrough Achievers

No journey is meant to be taken alone. As much as your personal growth is commendable, lasting change often comes from being part of a supportive community. You're now invited to join a community of breakthrough achievers—people who are committed to living intentionally, prioritizing what matters, and making meaningful strides in their careers and personal lives.

- **A Network of Like-Minded Individuals**: Communities are powerful because they offer accountability, encouragement, and shared wisdom. By connecting with others who are on similar paths, you reinforce your own commitment to growth. This network isn't about competition; it's about collaboration and celebrating each other's wins. Imagine being surrounded by people who understand the challenges you face and who are equally invested in making breakthroughs happen.

- **Growth Beyond the Book**: Joining the community extends the learning and growth beyond the pages of this book. It's an ongoing journey, where you can share your experiences, learn from the breakthroughs of others, and continue to evolve your approach. Personal development is never a one-and-done effort—it's a lifelong pursuit. Engaging with others helps keep that momentum alive.

- **The Power of Collective Breakthroughs**: There's something incredibly powerful about collective breakthroughs. When individuals come together with a shared mission, their combined energy can create massive shifts. Whether it's sharing tips for prioritization, brainstorming ways to overcome new blockers, or simply offering support during challenging times, being part of this community will amplify your efforts.

Leaving a Legacy of Clarity and Focus

As you reflect on your journey, consider the legacy you're leaving. Legacy isn't just about what you achieve—it's about the impact you have on others and the ideas you champion. By choosing clarity, focus, and meaningful action, you're contributing to a new way of working and living that values depth over breadth and quality over quantity.

- **Redefining Success**: You've redefined what success looks like. It's no longer about being busy for the sake of being busy. Instead, it's about making deliberate choices that align with your highest aspirations. This new definition of success is one that others will be inspired to adopt, as they see the tangible difference it makes in your life.

- **The Legacy of Focused Action**: Imagine the impact of a world where more people operated from a place of focus and clarity—where professionals were not overwhelmed but empowered, where leaders made decisions based on what truly matters, and where individuals felt fulfilled rather than drained. Your journey is a step towards that vision. Every time you choose to prioritize, to eliminate the unnecessary, and to act with intention, you're not just making a difference for yourself—you're contributing to a broader shift in how we work and live.

- **Inspiring Future Generations**: Think about the future professionals—the young people who are just starting their careers. They're watching and learning from those who came before them. By leading with clarity and focus, you're setting a precedent for what effective, fulfilling work can look like. You're demonstrating that it's possible to be successful without succumbing to constant busyness, and that's a powerful message for the next generation.

The Journey Forward

As we bring this chapter, and this book, to a close, it's important to acknowledge that your journey forward is filled with possibility. You now have the tools and the mindset to continue making breakthroughs. The CLEAR framework is yours to use, adapt, and refine as you face new challenges and opportunities. Remember, the purpose of these tools isn't to be rigid rules—they're meant to serve you, to evolve with you as you grow.

- **Commitment to Continuous Improvement**: Growth doesn't stop here. You've learned how to categorize, eliminate, prioritize, and act, but there will always be new blockers and new complexities. That's okay. The goal isn't to eliminate every challenge, but to become adept at navigating them. Commit to revisiting these principles regularly and to staying curious about how they apply to your ever-changing context.

- **Embrace New Challenges**: Don't shy away from the next challenge. Every breakthrough you've made so far has come from leaning into discomfort, embracing the unknown, and trusting in your ability to figure it out. Whether it's a career transition, a major project, or a new role, the same principles of focus, clarity, and strategic action will guide you.

- **Share Your Story**: Lastly, don't underestimate the power of sharing your story. The breakthroughs you've experienced have the potential to inspire others who are where you once were—struggling with overwhelm, unsure of where to start. Share your journey, not as someone who has it all figured out, but as someone who has faced challenges, learned, and grown. Your story matters, and it might just be the encouragement someone else needs to start their own journey.

Conclusion: The Ripple Never Ends

The journey you've embarked on is about more than achieving career success—it's about transforming how you approach life. It's about choosing what matters, releasing what doesn't, and moving forward with intention. This journey has no endpoint, because growth is continuous, and every breakthrough creates the potential for another.

As you close this book, take a deep breath and appreciate how far you've come. Remember that every step you take towards clarity and focus brings you closer to your goals and makes a difference not only in your own life but also in the lives of those around you. You're not just shaping your career—you're creating a legacy of intentional living, focused growth, and meaningful success.

Continue Your Breakthroughs...

You are now ready to continue your journey toward achieving breakthroughs. Explore ways to use AI-powered tools to research the latest information, practical tips, and insights tailored to your niche, line of work, or career. By leveraging AI, you can stay updated, uncover strategies, and find resources to fuel your personal progress and breakthroughs. Remember to stay focused – and continue to prioritize and ignore for maximum success going forward. Let's keep making progress together!

Connect & Inspire...

I thank you for embarking on this journey with me to escape the overwhelm trap and unlock your true potential. If you found value in Breakthroughology, I would greatly appreciate it if you'd take a moment to share your insights by leaving a review. Your feedback is invaluable in helping other true achievers and entrepreneurs discover these transformative principles and life-changing methods. One review from you could be the lifeline someone needs. Right now, they're drowning in tasks – just like you once were. Thank you.

Go here to leave your review:

https://breakthroughologybook.com/reviews

"It's not about having time, it's about making time."
– Unknown

Chapter Twenty

Appendices

Worksheet Creation Guide

Your breakthrough journey continues with these resources that will help you create practical, personalized worksheets to implement the strategies we've discussed throughout the book. These appendices will guide you through creating your own toolset—starting with the Breakthrough Blocker Test and continuing through the CLEAR framework worksheets. You'll also find recommendations for further growth resources.

Think of these appendices as your blueprint for building a personal toolbelt. Each section will provide detailed instructions for creating worksheets tailored to your specific needs and circumstances. By creating your own worksheets, you'll be able to customize them to your situation and modify them as you grow.

Appendix A:

Creating Your Breakthrough Blocker Test Worksheet

The Breakthrough Blocker Test will be your personal gatekeeper against distractions. This guide will help you create a decision-making tool that works specifically for you.

Think of your professional life as a garden—each task competing for your time and energy like plants competing for sunlight. Your worksheet will help you decide which "plants" to nurture and which to remove, focusing your attention on what truly deserves to flourish.

Setting Up Your Worksheet

Create a document with four main sections:

1. Task Inventory Section
- Create a wide column for listing all tasks
- Add columns for date, priority level, and decision
- Leave ample space for notes and reflections

2. Categorization Grid
- Draw a grid with sections for:
* Essential tasks

* Potential delegations
* Elimination candidates
- Include checkboxes next to each entry

3. Decision Framework
- Create a flowchart-style section with three questions:
* "Does this align with my core goals?"
* "Is this moving me toward a breakthrough?"
* "Is this merely occupying time?"
- Add yes/no branches after each question

4. Action Plan
- Create three columns:
* Keep (with explanation)
* Delegate (with to whom)
* Eliminate (with timeline)

Example of the Four Parts of Your Worksheet...

Task Inventory Section

Task Description	Date	Priority Level	Decision	Notes and Reflections

Categorization Grid

Essential Tasks	Potential Delegations	Elimination Candidates

Decision Framework

Flowchart Questions:

1. Does this align with my core goal?
   [ ] Yes
   [ ] No

2. Is this moving me toward a breakthrough?
   [ ] Yes
   [ ] No

3. Is this merely occupying time?
   [ ] Yes
   [ ] No

Action Plan

Keep (with explanation)	Delegate (with to whom)	Eliminate (with timeline)

Using Your Worksheet

1. List every task, project, and responsibility
2. Apply the CLEAR framework categorization
3. Run each item through your decision framework
4. Document your decisions and next steps

Remember to leave space for regular review and adjustments as your priorities evolve.

Appendix B:

Creating Your CLEAR Framework Worksheets

Transform the CLEAR framework concepts into actionable tools by creating your own set of personalized worksheets. Each worksheet will help you move from theory to practice, giving you concrete ways to implement what you've learned.

1. Creating Your Categorize Worksheet

Design a worksheet with these sections:

1. Task Inventory
- Create a comprehensive list section
- Add columns for:
* Task description
* Category assignment
* Impact level
* Notes

2. Category Definitions
Create sections for:
- Essential Tasks (directly align with goals)
- Supportive Tasks (indirect contributions)

- Delegatable Tasks (can be done by others)
- Filler Tasks (busy work)
- Eliminatable Tasks (time-wasters)

3. Reflection Space

Add prompts like:

- "Why is this task in this category?"
- "Could this task be moved to a different category?"
- "What patterns do I notice in my task distribution?"

Examples of CLEAR Framework Worksheets...

Categories – Task Inventory

Task Description	Category Assignment	Impact Level	Notes

Category Definitions

Essential Tasks (directly align with goals)	Supportive Tasks (indirect contributions)	Delegatable Tasks (can be done by others)	Filler Tasks (busy work)	Eliminatable Tasks (time wasters)

Reflection Space

Why is this task in this category?
Could this task be moved to a different category?
What patterns do I notice in my task distribution?

2. Creating Your List Priorities Worksheet

Design this worksheet with:

1. Core Goals Section
- Space to list long-term career goals
- Supporting activities for each goal
- Priority ranking system (High/Medium/Low)

2. Time and Energy Assessment
Create columns for:
- Goal/Activity
- Time required
- Energy level needed
- Impact rating

3. North Star Alignment Check
Include reflection questions:
- "Does this priority align with my breakthrough goals?"
- "What am I prioritizing that doesn't serve my goals?"
- "Which tasks need higher priority?"

Samples of the List Priorities Worksheets...

Core Goals Section

Long-Term Career Goals	Supporting Activities for Goal	Priority (High/Medium/Low)

Time and Energy Assessment

Goal/Activity	Time Required	Energy Level Needed	Impact Rating

North Star Alignment Check

Does this priority align with my breakthrough goals?
What am I prioritizing that doesn't serve my goals?
Which tasks need higher priority?

3. Creating Your Eliminate Worksheet

Structure this worksheet with:

1. Task Evaluation Grid

Create columns for:

- Current tasks

- Value assessment

- Delegation potential

- Keep/Delegate/Eliminate decision
- Action steps

2. Elimination Filter Questions

Include prompts like:
- "What happens if I stop doing this?"
- "Who could take this over?"
- "Why am I holding onto this?"

Samples of Eliminate Worksheets...

Task Evaluation Grid

Current Tasks	Value Assessment	Delegation Potential	Keep/Delegate/Eliminate Decision	Action Steps

Eliminate Filter Questions

What happens if I stop doing this?
Who could take this over?
Why am I holding onto this?

4. Creating Your Act Plan Template

Design this template with:

1. Goal Breakdown Section

Include spaces for:

- Specific goal description
- Milestone markers
- Action steps for each milestone
- Deadlines
- Required resources

2. Progress Tracking

Create columns for:

- Action item
- Deadline
- Status
- Obstacles
- Solutions

Samples of An Act Plan...

Goal Breakdown Section

Specific Goal Description
Milestone Markers
Action Steps for Each Milestone
Deadlines
Required Resources

Progress Tracking

Action Item	Deadline	Status	Obstacles	Solutions

5. Creating Your Refine Reflection Sheet

Design this sheet with:

1. Progress Review Section
Include spaces for:
- Achievements
- Challenges
- Lessons learned
- Adjustments needed

2. Strategy Assessment

Add prompts like:

- "What's working well?"
- "What needs to change?"
- "How can I improve my approach?"

Samples of a Refine Reflection Template Sheet...

Progress Review Section

Achievements
Challenges
Lessons Learned
Adjustments Needed

Strategy Assessment

What's Working Well?
What Needs to Change?
How Can I Improve My Approach?

Remember to leave ample space in each worksheet for writing and reflection. You may want to create both print and digital versions to suit different working styles and situations.

Appendix C:

Creating Your Personal Growth Resource Library

Transform these recommendations into your own curated resource collection that aligns with your breakthrough journey. Here's how to build and organize your personal development library:

Setting Up Your Resource Database

Create a document or digital system with these sections:

1. Reading List

Create categories for:

- Core breakthrough concepts
- Productivity and focus
- Habit formation
- Career development

For each resource, include spaces to note:

- Key takeaways
- Action items

- Implementation ideas
- Personal reflections

2. Learning Resources Grid

Organize by type:

- Books
- Articles
- Podcasts
- Tools

Include columns for:

- Resource name
- Main focus area
- Key benefits
- Priority level
- Status (completed/in progress)

3. Implementation Tracker

Create sections to monitor:

- Tools you're testing
- Methods you're implementing
- Results and observations
- Adjustments needed

Suggested Categories to Include

1. Focus & Productivity
- Deep work strategies
- Distraction elimination
- Time management

2. Habit Building
- Small changes implementation
- Progress tracking
- Behavior modification

3. Professional Development
- Career growth
- Leadership skills
- Industry innovation

4. Tools & Technology
- Productivity apps
- Organization systems
- Focus enhancers

Remember to:
- Update your resource library regularly
- Track which resources provide the most value
- Note specific applications to your situation
- Schedule regular review and reflection time

Appendix D:

Recommended Resources for Continuous Growth

True breakthroughs are built on continuous learning and growth.

This appendix is a curated list of books, articles, podcasts, and tools that are meant to extend your learning journey. The materials selected here have been chosen specifically because they resonate with the themes of Breakthroughology—clarity, focus, prioritization, and career transformation. The goal is for you to have go-to resources whenever you feel the need for a dose of inspiration, motivation, or even a push back on track.

Books to Deepen Your Understanding

- **"Essentialism" by Greg McKeown**: Dive deeper into the power of doing less but better. This book expands on the idea that it's only by cutting out the trivial that we make space for the truly significant.
- **"Deep Work" by Cal Newport**: Newport's perspective on focus aligns perfectly with the Breakthrough Blocker Method. It offers insights into structuring your time to produce high-quality, meaningful work.

- **"Atomic Habits" by James Clear**: A practical guide on how small, incremental changes can lead to massive improvements over time. This complements the idea of refining your processes in the CLEAR framework.

Articles and Papers for Quick Insights

- **"The Cost of Interrupted Work: More Speed and Stress" by Gloria Mark**: This research-based article dives into how interruptions can severely hamper productivity, providing further backing for the importance of eliminating distractions.
- **"How Successful People Spend Their Weekends" (Harvard Business Review)**: A powerful reminder that true productivity also involves strategic rest and recharge—essential for sustainable breakthroughs.

Podcasts to Keep You Inspired

- **"The Tim Ferriss Show"**: Ferriss often interviews world-class performers who share their experiences with productivity, focus, and work-life integration.
- **"Focus on This"**: Hosted by productivity experts, this podcast provides actionable tips on improving focus and effectiveness in both professional and personal spheres.

Tools to Support Ongoing Breakthroughs

- **Notion**: A versatile tool that can help you organize your thoughts, track your progress, and keep all of your Breakthrough Blocker Test insights in one place.
- **Trello**: Perfect for categorizing and prioritizing tasks using visual boards, especially helpful for implementing the CLEAR framework.
- **Pomodoro Timer**: Simple but effective, the Pomodoro technique helps in staying focused and breaking work into manageable chunks, making it easier to tackle priority actions without burning out.

This appendix closes with a reminder that breakthroughs don't happen in isolation. They're a result of an ongoing commitment to learning, refining, and engaging with tools and ideas that push you forward. The resources here are meant to keep you inspired, informed, and ready for whatever comes next.

Moving Forward

As you complete these appendices, you're not just wrapping up this book—you're setting the stage for a lifetime of breakthroughs. The key to sustained growth lies in using the right tools, maintaining an adaptable mindset, and constantly reaching for new knowledge. Armed with these frameworks and insights, you're now equipped to create meaningful change not just in your career, but as a catalyst for industry innovation and leadership. You have everything you need to become a force of change beyond yourself.

"Efficiency is doing better what is already being done. Effectiveness is deciding what to do better."

- Peter Drucker
(Management consultant and author)

You've Read the Book—Now Let's Change Your Life

Dive deeper into transforming your life. Stay up to date with the latest tips, resources, and insights to continue growing and improving in every area of your life. Use the latest AI platform or tool to access valuable information that can help you take the next step toward your goals—whether it's at work, at home, or just for YOU.

Here's some areas you might like to research and keep updated on:

Work and Productivity:

Time management, work-life balance, AI developments, and tools for personal and professional growth.

Health and Wellness:

Natural stress relief alternatives, exercise routines, health tips, and strategies to keep your mind and body in top shape.

Family and Lifestyle:

Family activities, travel tips, logistics hacks, and ways to simplify and enjoy life with your loved ones.

And much more...

Utilize AI to maximize your success and unlock exclusive content, tips, and ideas!

Your review of Breakthroughology would be greatly appreciated:

https://breakthroughologybook.com/reviews

Thank you.

Cheers...

Made in United States
Troutdale, OR
03/22/2025

29952731R00142